TOULOUSE-LAUTREC'S
TABLE

Styling
Lydia Fasoli

Food styling
Marianne Paquin

Translation
Alex Campbell (main text)
Deborah Roberts (recipes)

Edited and designed
by Sylvie Raulet

Manufactured in Germany

98765432 First US edition
24689753
23456789

TOULOUSE-LAUTREC'S TABLE

Geneviève Diego-Dortignac
Jean-Bernard Naudin
and André Daguin

Random House - New York

CONTENTS

AU BAR, *1887.*
Page 6 : Toulouse-Lautrec's love of food
and drink did not extend to water : he disliked the taste
and discouraged his table companions from imbibing it by
putting goldfish in the carafes of water.

HENRI de Toulouse-Lautrec was a giant, a colossus in the world of art, larger than life in all he did and a great cook as he was a great painter.

Creative, innovative, daring, he had great moral stature.

He was bold in his painting, bold in his constant practical jokes, and yet he lacked the physical strength to protect himself from the reactions of his victims.

He applied color to his art in the same spirit as he added seasoning in his cooking : expansively, generously, but in just the right measure.

This is how he is seen by the people of southern France, to whom I am proud to belong.

Henri de Toulouse-Lautrec died at the beginning of this century, but we still feel his presence among us as we look at his painting, taste his recipes; he has left us the keys to his two secret gardens, which are now open to all.

André Daguin

Chapter 1

Childhood :
an education
in taste

*Between riding and games of croquet, Latin translations
and English lessons, the young Henri was brought up to
live the life of an aristocrat.*

ON the evening of November 24, 1864, the heavens went wild. Rain streamed down the windows of the Hôtel du Bosc in Albi, a large two-storied house that seemed to hide behind its seventeenth-century façade. Henri de Toulouse-Lautrec-Monfa was born late that night in this dwelling, which bore the name of his great-aunts, Joséphine and Eugénie, the two unmarried Du Bosc ladies who lived there.

Henri's mother Adèle, née Tapié de Céleyran, a virtuous woman of fortune, came from a family with a shrewd business sense who owned the finest estate in Narbonne. Their forebears had come from Italy in the fifteenth century, leaving their name, legend relates, to the snow-covered crests of the Valle d'Aosta. They distinguished themselves in the seventeenth century as officers and royal guards. In the eighteenth century some of them purchased the office of Président Trésorier Général, or chief minister to the treasury of France, which raised them to the ranks of the nobility. Hand in hand with its great wealth, the family was highly cultured. Adèle herself excelled at Latin literature and spoke fluent English, accomplishments that were then highly esteemed. She also shared the taste for good living of the provincial upper classes of the time — a taste she passed on to her son.

Descended from a cadet branch of the counts of Toulouse, Henri's father, Alphonse de Toulouse-Lautrec, belonged to an aristocratic family that had made its mark on French history. His ancestors numbered dukes of Aquitaine, of Gotland, and of Septimania, the marquis of Provence, princes of Baux and of Tripoli. Their abundant wealth, fabled in old Europe, lay scattered between the tranquil Loire and fiery Spain. Their women bore fairy-tale names : Mahaud of Sicily, Elvire of Castile, Jeanne of England, while they themselves traced a fascinating genealogical line of valiant knights and distinguished governors. Some fought against the pope, others gave their daughters to kings in marriage. Later came generations of captains and other notables, all of them superb huntsmen. This illus-

Previous double page : a glorious afternoon under the chestnut trees at the Hôtel du Bosc. Whatever their different daily pursuits, the Toulouse-Lautrec «clan» would gather in the garden around a table of cold drinks. The little Henri de Toulouse-Lautrec-Monfa, a lively and charming child, was nicknamed «Petit Bijou,» or «Little Jewel,» by his family.

Henri painted this portrait of his mother, Countess Adèle, in 1882. Throughout his life, she was his strongest support, his refuge. Mother and son kept up a regular correspondence, unusually informal for the period and sprinkled with English expressions : «Farewell, my dear, embrace the grannies and other ornaments to our family tree and believe me, Yours, Henri.

trious ancestry, with its rich variety of characters, left its mark on Lautrec, influencing the way he shaped his own extraordinary destiny.

The Toulouse-Lautrec and Tapié de Céleyran families were closely linked : Gabrielle, Henri's paternal grandmother, and Louise, his maternal grandmother, were sisters. And the upright Adèle, succumbing to the charms of the dashing Alphonse, a cavalry lieutenant, had married her first cousin. Everyone had rejoiced in a match that not only brought the families closer but enlarged their inheritance without blemish to the family coat of arms. No one envisaged the disastrous hereditary consequences of the intermarriage.

Nothing was run-of-the-mill in the life of the Toulouse-Lautrecs. They nevertheless respected what was proper to their social position, being conservative, fervent Catholics, and legitimist — to the point that they decided to call their firstborn son Henri, in tribute to Henri V, Count of Chambord. Last in the line descended from Louis XV, he had been supplanted on the French throne by Louis-Philippe and then Napoleon III. Henri's baptism was accorded all the ceremony due to an anointing. The newborn baby wore a family christening robe of fine muslin covered in embroidery, and a bonnet shaped like a crown.

« In our family, » said Alphonse lightheartedly, « we baptize at once... in the saddle ! » The boy continued to be exquisitely dressed, in costumes of his mother's choosing : velvet dresses, Scottish kilts, and sailor suits. But this did not stop him from putting into practice his father's principles. Alphonse was a dilettante with exquisite manners and an accomplished horseman, who had won numerous steeplechases and cross-country races. He was also a nonconformist with the whims of a spoiled child, renowned for his extravagant behavior. His eccentricities were legendary. One summer day Count Alphonse left for his native southwest, to visit the house in Albi that he owned jointly with his brother Charles. Splendidly attired in a dark suit, which did full justice to his elegant figure, he took his place in a first-class compartment of the train. While his trunks traveled in the luggage car, he kept with him his two constant companions : a cormorant for fishing and an eagle owl for the hunt. The journey was long, the af-

ternoon intensely hot. Stifled by the temperature, Alphonse took off his jacket and waistcoat, then his pants and vest, keeping on only his underwear. He next had the preposterous idea of hanging his clothes outside the carriage to air them. The wind, needless to say, swept them away...

Very properly attired in a stiff collar, his bowler hat pulled low over his brow, Charles was at the station to meet his older brother. He found the latter perfectly relaxed, dressed only in his underpants, the cormorant's basket secured to his back, the eagle owl's cage gripped in his hand. The general stupefaction can be imagined : amid the chaos of the station platforms, thronged with curious locals come to gape at the trains, the two men drew crowds and caused widespread amusement. Alphonse, for his part, was indignant at the wretched condition of the horse and carriage awaiting him : « I shall walk to the house ; I could never let myself be pulled by a nag like that. » A fierce argument followed, but was happily brought to a resolution : Alphonse installed himself comfortably on the carriage bench with his animals, while Charles sat cramped on the tip-up seat. The party set off, at a trot, for the Hôtel du Bosc.

The town of Albi is a play of color : all the shades of earth dried in the sun of the Midi. The faintest hint of saffron in the clay gives the brick its fine shade of red ocher, reminiscent of Italy. The houses turn russet in the sunshine ; the *Lices* — shaded avenues in the south of France — provide cool in the midday heat ; the streets wind their way toward the ramparts ; the townspeople are friendly. Below runs the temperamental river Tarn, swelling to a torrent of copper-colored water after heavy rain, subsiding at the height of summer. Here, in the fourteenth century, the archbishops built a fortified cathedral. Their own residence was La Berbie, a palace set amid hanging gardens by the river, planted with roses and cypress trees.

In the mid-nineteenth century massive building projects were undertaken in Paris under the direction of Baron Haussmann, inspiring similar development in the provinces. Albi did not escape the drive to modernize, acquiring a new bridge and major thoroughfares. Businesses and café terraces sprung up on the

Henri's father, Count Alphonse de Toulouse-Lautrec. Eccentric, elegant, and something of a dandy, he was always in pursuit of unusual experiences. On his morning outing in the Bois de Boulogne, he used to drive a Norwegian cart pulled by a Shetland pony. What struck others as extravagant behavior was to him an appreciation of style.

Place du Vigan in the heart of the old town. A few yards away, in the rue École-Mage, stood the house in which Henri was born.

It is said that houses shape the lives of those who live in them. Even though he never spent long periods there, the drawing room of the Hôtel du Bosc, a harmonious blend of the styles of Languedoc and the Age of Enlightenment, was to determine Henri's fate. When he was fourteen years old, he fell from a low chair in this great room, closely hung with portraits of his ancestors and opening on to terraces. A careless fracture brought to light an incurable inherited condition and put an end to his riding days. The boy's fragile legs stopped growing and he was crippled for the rest of his life. He was just under five feet tall.

On the garden side, the house, dignified by its crenelated tower, had enormous charm. A series of terraces edged with lilac, box hedges, and laburnum, and buttressed by the town ramparts, descended to the Bondidou gully. When Henri was not amusing himself bathing cormorants in the ponds, he spent happy hours with his father in overgrown corners of the moat. The two of them would hide in the bushes and put into practice the lessons in Georges de Buffon's *Natural History*. They observed the behavior of birds, the movements of wrens and warblers, the repetitive routine of the tits. They identified the plumage of the different species and their various nests.

In fact, however, when he was in Albi, Henri did not see a great deal of his father. Elusive, and utterly original, a trait he passed on to his son, Alphonse insisted on living in the crenelated tower with his birds of prey, denying entrance to all comers. He had a pulley system fitted at a window of his lofty retreat, by means of which food was sent up to him in a basket on the end of a rope. Woe betide the worthy Léon — the coachman entrusted with the task — if he inadvertently failed to cater for the needs of the hungry birds. A careless mistake was tantamount to an international incident. « I find it unacceptable that he is capable of mistaking a rat for a mouse ! My eagle owl is not a native of Thuringia, where his kind will eat anything. He was born in the Périgord, where animals and humans are used to high-quality food, » complained Alphonse

Art and the horse dominated Lautrec's childhood. He learned to ride under the watchful eye of his father. This drawing was done by René Princeteau, a well-known academic painter in Paris and a family friend. He followed Henri's artistic career in later life and gave him advice.

Summer 1896. This family photograph was taken in the courtyard of the Hôtel du Bosc by the Abbé Peyre, tutor to the boys. Henri was then thirty-two years old. With him are his cousin Marie, a future photographer; his two grandmothers, Louise and Gabrielle; his uncles, wearing boaters; his aunts, looking a little starchy; and a string of cousins. Tuck, the highly respectable bulldog, was very much a part of château life.

The *Château du Bosc, set
in the rough countryside of
Rouergue, had been the
family «fortress» for over
seven centuries. Over the
years, trees, flowers, and
lawns had taken over the
moat. More attracted to
nineteenth-century comfort
than feudal austerity,
Gabrielle de Toulouse-
Lautrec, Henri's
grandmother, renovated the
interior and opened
windows in the virtually
blank walls, giving new life
to the building without
changing the family
traditions.*

in a note to Charles, delivered by means of the basket.

Henri always looked forward to the visits of his great-grandmother Adèle de La Roque-Bouillac. Nicknamed « Monkey's Granny » by Henri, she lived with a pack of monkeys and baboons. In her old age only one of them survived : a long-tailed monkey called Julia, from whom she was inseparable. Julia filled the role of companion ; anyone wanting to please her mistress had to pay court to her. She would simper at the slightest compliment, nibble sweets, play with a fan, respond to politenesses, and listen to conversations, showing particular interest in what Adèle had to say — as often as not an interminable speech on the « Yellow Peril » at the gates, or the Russian advance into Europe.

At lunch, Julia would take precedence over the guests, and the meal proceeded according to a clearly defined ritual. Not until she was seated in the place of honor, her napkin around her neck, did the servants start to pass the dishes. The monkey was well versed in the art of fine living, and skillfully handled the cutlery engraved with the Toulouse-Lautrec crest. She appreciated a Château La Barde wine, particularly when it was served in a silver cup. After the meal, and a postprandial stroll in the garden, she would perch on her mistress's shoulder.

In later life Henri remembered the garden as a natural theater, the venue of unusual, exotic, even fantastical happenings. His father once organized a flight of multicolored kites across the skies of Albi, watched by the marveling eyes of the children pulling the strings. Several carpenters were employed for the occasion to cut, glue, and nail the wooden kite frames, which were as light as those made by the Japanese.

Henri led a sheltered childhood, divided between lessons and carefree hours. Life on the family's ancestral lands followed its own rhythm, free of the everyday constraints of the rest of the world. One of the main activities was hunting, which had reached its high point in France in the reign of Louis XV. Count Alphonse, an accomplished horseman, took to it with zeal : he was the roaming southerner in the mists of the Sologne, captivated by the forests of Orléans with their abundant game. He loved setting out at daybreak from his country house at Loury-sous-Bois, when the whippers-in arrived with the hounds, after the ritual repast copiously washed down with local wine. This passion for the hunt was handed down in the Lautrec family from father to son, together with the love of good food, which Henri was to inherit.

More drawn to Mediterranean skies than the milder charms of the Loiret, where she had never truly felt at home, Henri's mother eventually left Loury. This occurred a few years after the first tragedy of her married life, the death in 1868 of her second son, Richard, at age one. Signs of a rift between husband and wife were emerging. While in many ways a splendid figure, Alphonse was both a fantasist and a womanizer — and undeniably difficult as a husband. A single anecdote sums up his character. Recently married, and on a visit to Nice with Adèle, he suddenly disappeared in the middle of dinner at the Negresco restaurant. Days went by, then weeks, without any news of him. His abandoned wife turned to her mother for consolation. Only two months later — which to his nomadic spirit might as easily have been two days — did a message reach Adèle at Loury. It was as peremptory as it was brief : « Send ferrets, » signed Alphonse.

The escapades of her fickle husband forged a remarkable strength of character in Adèle. She became an exemplary mother, patient, acute, selfless, and astonishingly self-controlled ; all of these qualities she combined with a shrewd business sense.

The couple drifted further and further apart. In 1872 the « Flower of Paradise, » as she was known in her circle, moved to Paris, using her son's education as an excuse to leave the country house at Loury where she had been so unhappy. Henri's poor health took them also to Nice and to Barèges, where he drew, between bouts of medical treatment, as a way of forgetting his illness. His father, meanwhile, returned to his falcons, his horses, and his eccentricities. The silence of the forests answered his sporadic need for solitude. At other times he presented himself to the world in a wide range of guises, from the most worldly to the most outlandish ; he would even milk his mare for breakfast in an avenue of the Bois de Boulogne. He made a habit of unconventional dress : one day he might deck himself out as a dandy in tailor-made

clothes from Savile Row in London, with shoes from Maxwell's or boots by Bunting; another, he might brave icy temperatures in a white flannel suit, or appear wearing a Buffalo Bill hat. Unless of course he was dressed as a samurai, a Scottish lord, or a knight in coat of mail... Whimsical and unpredictable, he freely indulged his every fancy — such as a sudden urge to execute half-turns on a Manchurian saddle, for the sheer aesthetic pleasure of it. His letters to his mother are scattered with references to his dress : « I am delighted with my Caucasian helmet, which is shaped like the towers of the Château du Bosc. »

The Château du Bosc, perfectly set in the severe landscape of Rouergue, was the paternal family seat lived in by Grandmama Gabrielle. Massively built to withstand attack, it had been a fortress in the twelfth century. From this period there survived two towers with loopholes, topped in mottled roofing stone. Gabrielle converted this austere edifice into a comfortable home habitable throughout the year — successfully resisting the current fashion for the neo-Gothic introduced by Viollet-le-Duc. Large windows were opened on every side to let in the sun, which penetrated even the darkest of rooms; bedrooms were installed in the attics.

The family, attended by a battalion of servants, pursued a timeless existence amid the trees, surrounded by books and ancestral portraits. Talented art lovers, they spent long hours drawing and painting in watercolor, and knew a number of academic and fashionable painters. Count Alphonse was a friend of Princeteau, who specialized in painting packs of hounds and riding scenes and shared his interest in animal subjects. The true key to family life, however, was a shared love of eating well. This prompted Gabrielle's observation : « When my sons kill a woodcock they are delighted three times over : once when they shoot it, once when they sketch it, once when they eat it ! »

Henri's first taste of good food was the cooking of Languedoc. Essentially robust in character, but refined by successive generations of his ancestors, it had acquired subtlety and succulence. Creative cooks, applying the culinary secrets of the house, managed to give the simplest of dishes an indefinable aristocratic touch.

The young Henri was presented with dishes both sub-

Left : a shooting scene in the forest. The shoots kept the cooks at the Château du Bosc well supplied with game and provided Henri, from early childhood, with subjects to sketch.

The Château du Bosc had two towers roofed in stone tiles which captured the imagination of Alphonse de Toulouse-Lautrec, who always had an eye for the unusual : « I am delighted with my Caucasian helmet, which is shaped like the towers of the Château du Bosc. »

19

The domestic staff of the Château du Bosc. The graciousness, the hospitality, the entire style of life at the château depended on the labors of cooks, governesses, nurses, maids, valets, drivers, and gardeners. Each time a baby was born, a nurse was engaged. According to Countess Attems, Henri's great-grandniece : « The domestic staff in the house were particularly numerous because each household brought their own servants to join grandmother's. » The letters Henri wrote to his grandmother as a child all mention the servants : « Tell me if Annou, Justine, and Antoine are well, » «Hello to Miss Rosette, » or again, «Remember me to Flavie, Mélanie, and Benjamin. »

Right : from the walls of the paneled dining room, ancestral portraits survey the feast. Whether a meal was simple or grand, whatever the number of guests, the table itself was unostentatious and was often decorated with a bunch of flowers. A pantry in the tower simplified the serving of meals, the kitchens being on the ground floor. The silver was polished in this little round room.

stantial and strongly flavored, combining « body » and « verve » — fricasees, salmis, sauces thickened with blood, goose liver, conserves, larded pheasant à la Périgueux (a recipe attributed to a great-grandfather), haunches of wild boar and venison dripping in rich brown gravy, and yet more game, prepared according to yet more recipes. The ancient methods of cooking on charcoal and the spit were also put to good use.

As a child, Henri spent most of his holidays at the Château du Bosc. Later, as « Uncle Henri, » he went there in the summer to relax « in the bosom of the family, » far from any reminders of his life in the shadier districts of Paris, of the world of circuses and music halls, and women in brothels, all of which provided the subjects of his art.

Among his childhood memories was an image of parasols crossing sandy avenues, light filtering through the leaves of chestnut trees. He recalled devising « hippopotamus traps » and other pieces of mischief ; signing letters to his mother « Phileas Fogg » at a period when he was voraciously reading Jules Verne ; designing a miniature Bois de Boulogne on the parkland where his cousins drove their horses and carriages ; and worrying lest a brougham carriage and dogcart fail to be delivered on time, while Augé, the Narbonne merchant entrusted with the order, did his utmost to find these English-made vehicles in Paris. On another occasion, after a donkey was bought, a variant on the dog break was improvised, and all the children piled in for a ride.

Everyone was an amateur botanist and entomologist. Under the pretext of observing beetles in the spongy moss, with gadgets cobbled together out of scraps of wood, or studying the work of the mason bees, or rescuing a nestling fallen from its nest, one could slip off to the woods of La Gravasse, out of range of the governess's watchful eye. Henri's uncles had shown him all the paths through the forest, tiny trails to find mushrooms, tracks penetrating the undergrowth. He went hunting there with his father and Grésigue the falcon, across tracts of rough hillside intersected by great ravines, where stones went hurtling into the void. Not far from there, the scree slopes of the Viaur river valley brought memories of his grand-

Previous double page : the children's favorite desserts; an apple tart and fresh fruits of the season. July brought cherries, which stained cloth and baskets on their route from orchard to table. Next came the very early Messire Saint-Jean pears.

Even on holiday, Lautrec kept some of his Parisian habits. One, among others, was the apéritif : a glass of port, on which he would sprinkle a little nutmeg.

Right : after dinner there was conversation in the drawing room, while the men drank liqueurs and the women herb tea. Count Alphonse did not always join in, preferring to read. Seated in a high-backed chair, which added to his air of distinction, he would immerse himself in one of his many volumes on falconry; though he knew them by heart, he never tired of them.

father, Count Raymond. One cold and misty winter day he had gone out shooting, his dogs at his heels, and had never come back. This happened in 1871, when Henri was age seven.

Hunting and shooting — on foot, with dogs, or with guns — had taken up most, if not all, of the days of Count Raymond's life. He was a familiar sight to the people of the area, accompanied by his pack of pale hounds, hunting hare in places known as « The Green Cross » and « The Bishop's Fountain. » He went stag hunting too, over the vast expanses of the Landes. Thin and aristocratic, black-haired, with piercing eyes, he was a conspicuous figure, known by the nickname «the Black Prince » after he attended a fancy dress ball wearing the somber armor of that legendary Prince of Wales. This, at any rate, was the story told to the children.

The first born of his generation, Henri enjoyed the privileges of being the eldest child, presiding over his fourteen first cousins in youth and into adulthood. The family used to foregather in the great drawing room hung with Aubusson tapestries. Ordered from Settelin, these had never left the walls for which they were made. Conversation flowed freely, art proving a much more popular topic than business. Political discussion never assumed very serious proportions in this family which, united by its own traditions, had long since turned its back on current events. But whatever the subject, the talk never lacked in wit and brilliance. In the evenings an atmosphere of peace reigned in the drawing room : the dogs curled up drowsily in front of the silk and mahogany fire screen, the grandmothers embroidered, and Alphonse buried himself for the umpteenth time in a book of falconry. Meanwhile, under his mother's tutelage, Henri was taught to read in English : the intellectual world of the period was decidedly anglophile. The language remained a close and lasting bond between mother and son.

The eclectic interior, on which each generation had left its mark, paid no serious attention to overall effect. With its Louis XIII chairs and Louis XIV chests of drawers, its plethora of animal bronzes and knick-knacks, the drawing room was a mixture of contemporary taste and serried inherited objects. Comfortable upholstered armchairs — more bourgeois than aristocratic in taste — were conducive both to afternoon naps and to conversation. Over the years, an extraordinary collection of photographs, in silver, lacquer, and leather frames, most of them taken by Cousin Marie, accumulated on console tables and mantelpieces.

Marie, who was seventeen years younger than Henri, shared his artistic temperament, and the two cousins were very much in sympathy with each other. She loved photographing everyday scenes of country life, children, animals, and servants, and would afterward disappear into a workroom in the outbuildings to busy herself over blue boxes of photographic plates coated with silver gelatin-bromide, a portable, folding darkroom — in short, all the equipment necessary for developing the images.

Henri meanwhile made his way with hobbling gait around the château. His riding days were over, and long walks tired him. He set up his easel by some wisteria, guelder roses, and rambling roses, the perfect background to his portraits. Nature itself was not a significant element in his work : he was much more interested in the study of a facial expression, the stance of a figure, the movement of an animal, or, for that matter, military exercises in the countryside. He believed, however, that natural light gave a special quality to faces.

On one of these summer visits, casting his mind back to the days of his childhood, he took a piece of charcoal from the fireplace and, encouraged by his uncle Charles, drew on the walls of the orangery all the familiar figures of his youth : dogs, trotting horsemen, and, in a quick and provocative sketch, Adeline, the Countess Adèle's companion, smoking a pipe.

Drawing, sketching, capturing a fleeting expression, always held a fascination for Henri. At the early age of four, when set to sign the register of his younger brother's baptism, he had been seized by the urge to sketch an ox. When not drawing, he played like any other child, willingly joining in rowdy fun and games. He loved puppets, built models of boats, and enjoyed dressing up. All ages used to mime scenes in front of the orangery. The tiniest corner of blue sky was sufficient pretext to take the chaise longues outside for an

Photography was the latest fashion. Portraits of family and friends littered chests of drawers and mantelpieces. Some bore the signature of Nadar, the brilliant photographer of artists and celebrities.

No one escaped Lautrec's
incisive pencil strokes, not
his uncles or cousins,
horsemen or huntsmen, not
even Adeline, Countess
Adèle's companion.

*Right : the young Lautrec's
«illustrative spark» found
an outlet on the walls of
the orangery, which was
used as a storeroom in the
summer. The painter, who
«amused himself in life
with the complete freedom
of a little boy in a garden
square,» as his friend
Maurice Joyant later said,
dashed off an entertaining
gallery of portraits.*

interval of refreshment. Glasses were set out on a table, and everyone made their choice of drink : blackberry syrup, orangeade, or orgeat syrup, all homemade. At tea the nannies served the children apple compote, flavored with vanilla pods and lemon rind. The days were interspersed with edible treats, fruits in homemade jelly, fritters dipped in sugar, not to mention « *galette de plomb* » (literally, lead griddle cake) to satisfy even the hungriest of appetites.

And so the days went by, carefree and unconstrained, with only the changing level of the sun on the horizon to mark the passage of time. The sole imposition was attendance at daily mass in a chapel built in 1880 on the edge of the park. Then autumn made its sudden arrival, enveloping all in morning mist. This meant the return to Paris for some, the start of the shooting season for others.

Get-togethers at the Château du Bosc began with the first glimmer of dawn, around a huge breakfast. The table was laid in the dining room and left in place for late risers. On the damask tablecloth, embroidered with the monogram « T.L., » the servants arranged the family china and silver around a generous assortment of sweetmeats and savories. There were jams cooked in copper pans, local honey the yellow of amber, well-risen brioches, plump boned hams, salted liver sausages, curving sausages, terrines, foie gras larded with truffles in goose fat, milk frothing fresh from the cow, coffee, and bottles of Céleyran wine. The finishing touches to this early-morning banquet were crusty loaves of bread rolled in flour, succulent fritters perfectly browned, chicken in aspic, vegetables from the garden, and hard cheeses. A generous plateful, to say the least.

The Sunday picnics made so fashionable by Edouard Manet's painting *Le Déjeuner sur l'herbe* were very popular with city dwellers deprived of rural life. Henri's family and their circle preferred more sporting expeditions that gave them an appetite for their alfresco meals. They set out equipped with folding chairs, fishing rods, and baskets, in which to collect — depending on the season — wild raspberries, wild cherries, blackberries, hazelnuts, mushrooms, or chestnuts. The picnic was laid out on a simple white cloth spread on the

Previous double page : breakfast was a substantial meal at the Château du Bosc. The table was laid at dawn for those going shooting, and left in place for those who got up late. Everyone helped themselves to what they wanted. There was coffee, bread and jam, fried eggs, sponge cake, tarts warm from the oven, fruit salad, and, for those with more robust appetites, sausages made from offal and little cubes of fat, boudin noir (black pudding), leg of pork, pâté,

fried crackling, and goose liver, plus an accompanying dish of vegetables, often flavored with the pink garlic of the Tarn valley.

There were occasional fishing expeditions. Here the party is seen heading for the Vergnasse stream, equipped from top to toe, baskets slung across their backs, rods over their shoulders. They took with them smoked hams, cured sausages, and fruit tarts in case of hunger.

grass : bacon omelette, pâté en croûte, chicken flavored with fragrant truffles, on which everyone fell with delight.

Nothing, however, could ever rival lunch in the paneled dining room, around the customary white damask tablecloth, finely embroidered or encrusted with lace, according to the occasion. There could be more than twenty-five members of the family and close friends seated at table but the cooks were never caught unawares. Lunch was served at midday and, without being inordinately prolonged, consisted of entrées, one or two main courses, side dishes, cheese, and dessert. Coffee was taken in the drawing room, followed by an eau-de-vie or Armagnac.

Meals in honor of the hunt and its patron Saint Hubert were always an excuse for a banquet. At the Château du Bosc the saint was commemorated many times throughout the year. Even if the hunt itself had lost seigneurial status after the Revolution, game remained highly popular at the Toulouse-Lautrecs' table, no other meat quite matching it for taste and aroma.

The kitchen of the château was a hive of activity from the early hours of the morning until late at night. It was run with the efficiency of a guardroom, with everything strategically placed in readiness for the great culinary maneuvers.

Rows of gleaming saucepans hung from a shelf, alongside their gleaming lids. Next to the ovens stood a series of cast-iron pots. There were great earthenware receptacles reserved for pork, pots or casseroles for simmering daubes and beans, and gratin dishes of baked clay in every shape and size, which were rubbed all over with garlic when new. By the chimney stood huge cauldrons, battered by use, trivets, and the dripping pan, which was placed under the spit to catch juices from the roasts. Finally came the molds and baking tins, used for cakes and tarts; copper pans, meticulously cleaned with vinegar and salt after fruit had been cooked in them; and a strange handmade contraption used to crush chestnuts for preserves.

The pace of work on the ground floor of the château was unimaginably hectic. Rose, the head cook, dedicated to pleasing her mistress, poured every effort into the preparation of meals, helped by kitchen maids act-

There were excellent traditional recipes to mark the occasion of a shoot. When a wild boar was killed, it was gutted and hung in one piece for several days. The haunch, the choice cut, was then marinated for a further three days in a glazed clay receptacle known as a grésale. Into the marinade went red wine, shallots, chopped onions and carrots, thyme, sage, bayleaf, pepper, and cloves. It made the meat tender and aromatic without masking its taste and, after being reduced and passed through a strainer, was used to make the accompanying sauce.

33

ing on her instructions. There were always fowls to pluck, vegetables to peel, mushrooms to clean, china to put away in the vast cupboards. But let anyone dare, without Rose's express instruction, interfere in any way with the hare à la royale... Without needing to taste every dish, she could tell the exact stage reached in cooking by a mere stir of her wooden spoon. Unrivaled in her roasting skills, she kept a close watch over the spit (which was turned by a dog), the frying, the croutons. An excellent pastry cook, she would flavor the simplest of cakes with a glass of house kirsch. On the pretext that alcohol entirely evaporated in cooking and that its flavor enriched the sauce, she used to pour a good dose of eau-de-vie on her rennet apples before putting them in the oven — the dessert was perfectly suitable for children! As were her *pascades*, thickish pancakes cooked in lard, which she kept in a drawer of the wooden table, her *oreillettes de la Chandeleur*, made for Candlemas day, and *gâteau à la broche*, which required very light handling.

Henri often used to watch the goings-on in the kitchen in preparation for forthcoming treats. He learned « the value of a grain of salt, » the succulence of a ragout, the felicitous associations of eel and truffle, and of omelette and saffron (a spice cultivated in former days by peasants in the Albi region and still used in a number of recipes); and also the sweeter delights of the desserts. He discovered the characteristic flavors of the region, developing an appreciation of food and an understanding of good cooking that became an important part of his life.

Rose was also responsible for the larder, the fruit, and the salted meat stores. These were cool, ventilated rooms next to the kitchen. The fruits were laid out on wooden slats to stop them going moldy. Medlars were set to ripen on straw, which gave them a very pleasant vinous flavor. With the quinces, picked in October, Rose made *poupets*, small rolls of bread enclosing the whole fruit, and *pâtes*, little fruit jellies, which Henri loved. Following local custom, quinces were also kept on a saucer in the linen cupboard for their fragrance. A room was reserved for cured and salted meats, hams, bacons, all kinds of sausages, stone jars of goose fat, and a specialty particularly

Left : quail is esteemed one of the most succulent meats. It is best simply roasted or cooked en papillote, as its aroma is fleeting and its delicate flavor would be lost in a sauce.

Cooks know a number of useful tricks for cooking game. Civet of hare, for example, is perfected by the addition to the wine sauce of pork rind and a piece of black chocolate to counteract the acidity of the alcohol. At the Château du Bosc dishes were systematically enhanced by the addition of garlic, or goose fat, or truffles.

35

Some of the table napkins were embroidered with the count's coronet above the monogram « T.B. ». This marked the alliance of two old French families, the Toulouses, whose peripatetic ancestors had taken part in the Crusades, and the Imberts du Bosc.
Previous double page : the monumental fireplace, built in the great hall in 1521, and bearing the arms of the Imbert du Bosc family, blazed with heat to welcome the hunters back from the chase.

Right : the best dinners at the Château du Bosc were perhaps those held for the shoots. They embodied a style of life, a respect for tradition, an aristocratic spirit, that Lautrec, however nonconformist he may have been, was never to forget. On these occasions the table was laid in the great hall, which had barely changed over the centuries apart from the addition of a billiard table in the second half of the nineteenth century.

popular with the men : salted pig's liver covered in pepper and tightly rolled in a cloth. Woodcock, brought back from the shoots, were hung from the beams for over a week to bring out their gamey taste and improve the texture of the meat. The poultry yard supplied corn-fed chickens, ducks, turkeys, and wonderfully tender capons. The farm provided calves ; the dairy, cheese. The more thoroughly the milk was drained and the greater the proportion of soured cream, the more melting was the cheese. It would alternatively be dried and left to stand in a jar of eau-de-vie.

Country life in a château required a minimum of fourteen domestic servants. The care of the silver was entrusted to Célestin, who polished it brilliantly with a magic black powder. In white gloves, solemn as a majordomo, he religiously laid out the gleaming pieces on the sideboards on the first floor. His wife, the ironing lady, operated a battery of irons of all shapes and sizes, kept in large cupboards in the laundry. At regular intervals, an ox-drawn cart would take linen and laundress to the river along the Pierrouche road. Family and friends, all generations mingling, followed the cart in happy procession — if only long enough to pose for the photographer.

Antoine, the indispensable gardener, grew a clever mixture of country flowers and more sophisticated blooms. The daffodil and tulip heralded spring, May brought the peony ; the nasturtium and convolvulus came with the summer. Roses gave fragrance in the hot months, stocks bloomed, even invading the paths. At the entrance to the château the gardener planted pampas grass, a particular favorite of Gabrielle's. The children made its fine and flexible stems into streamers. In one of the outbuildings behind the chapel, Antoine brought on roses in pots, stored bulbs and seeds, meticulously arranged in the drawers of a cabinet he had made. Only after he had tended thoroughly to the flowers would he proceed to one of the two vegetable gardens : the « lower garden » to the south, or the « seed bed, » which covered 2 1/4 acres by the farm. Whenever Antoine was asked how he divided the planting of the two gardens, he replied : « I do everything in both places. » There was, indeed, every vari-

Every morning a chaplain celebrated mass at the Château du Bosc. Starting in 1880, religious holidays and the births and marriages of successive generations of the family were celebrated in a chapel built on the edge of the park. These were also the occasions of family banquets.

Right : the traditional dessert of Rouergue. This cake cooked on a spit required great dexterity and patience, and involved two hours' preparation. But the results were spectacular.

ety of vegetable in each of the two gardens, though only the « seed bed » had a sizable orchard.

All his knowledge of wine and varieties of grape Henri acquired from 1872 onward, staying at Céleyran with his uncle Amédée in an Italianate villa surrounded by vineyards. The rough, stony soil produced a « raw » Mediterranean wine. In summer, temperatures approached ninety-five degrees Fahrenheit. There were extensive farm buildings on the estate, and magnificent stables able to accommodate over fifty horses.

An avenue of umbrella pines led to the château. One entered the main courtyard through a monumental gateway, giving on to orange trees planted in bowls from Anduze, oleanders, giant aloes, and palm trees set around an ornamental pond. Two square towers with balusters flanked the long, elegant façade, with its eaves of glazed clay and its seventeenth-century wrought-iron balcony.

Henri's holidays at Céleyran were an escape to paradise, to a world of natural luxury and careless ease. A path led to an idyllic walled garden, where one could pick huge bunches of violets, where for most of the winter Marie-Antoinette roses were in flower, with their unique purplish tint and scent of amber. Behind the house, hidden by the luxuriant vegetation, were greenhouses, emitting the heady scents of heliotrope and jasmine. The path to the chapel crossed a bridge over the water lilies.

Life with Uncle Amédée was carefree, and Lautrec felt utterly at home there. Carts laden with vats, groups of wine harvesters in the vineyards, which were flooded to combat phylloxera, coopers in the farmyard, all provided inspiration for Henri's first paintings.

Amédée's automobiles caused a great stir in the family. A keen follower of fashion, carried away by the tide of modernism, he developed a craze for racing cars, each successive model better than the one before. These new toys fascinated young and old alike. The crunch of wheels on the drive, the purr of an engine, brought everyone running. Was the model a vis-à-vis or a tonneau ? Made by Panhard or De Dion ? In the 1890s one of Henri's first cousins drove a flamboyant red convertible, its interior upholstered in gold-

Céleyran was an oasis of luxuriant vegetation amid the Mediterranean vineyards, a place where time seemed to stand still, where palm trees cast their shadows on the façade overlooking the front courtyard, and the scent of roses and orange trees escaped from the greenhouses. Henri came here first as a boy to spend his spring holidays with uncles, aunts, and cousins, playing among the flowers and ornamental ponds.

en yellow. The family gave every car a name, as if they had been horses : Blanchette, Bolet, Serpolet. Henri, who was forbidden to drive the newfangled monsters, sat astride the Bollé tri-car instead, his short legs dangling in empty space.

When he first visited Malromé, his mother's château — where he was ultimately to die — Henri was already a young man of nineteen, embarked on his bohemian life in Paris. The estate lay in the Bordeaux area, on the wine-growing soil of Entre-Deux-Mers : its white wine was sweet, sometimes almost like liqueur, its red wine full-bodied and strong-flavored. Adèle had bought the vineyard in May 1883, a move she explained thus : « Alphonse fully understands that I want to be 'at home' after twenty years of wandering. »

Straight away she engaged a manager called Balade, intending to replant 84 acres with American stock. But phylloxera unfortunately began to ravage the vines.

Henri came to Malromé in search of calm ; the place seemed imbued with a wise serenity, and in his mother's company he was able to rest and relax. No one in the area knew very much about him, and what they did know was merely that his paintings were « bizarre » : lots of rouged women, streetwalkers, cabaret dancers. Adèle was an excellent hostess. Hospitality to her was more than a question of good manners ; it was an expression of affection. She welcomed her son's friends with instinctive kindness, preparing all kinds of delicacies for them. Knowing their taste for good food, she served them a daube of marinated beef simmered long and slow, which Lautrec called « bœuf à la Malromé. » Alternatively, she offered them artichokes from the garden with oil and garlic, followed by cod à la biscaienne. Another specialty was the « serpent du couvent, » the « convent snake, » a sinfully delicious dessert covered in almond slivers. Henri was greatly amused that it was a nun, his mother's friend Sister Sainte-Léoncie, who had introduced her to the dish.

Lautrec was in the habit of ordering wine from his mother's estate, as the correspondence between mother and son bears witness : « Tell Balade to get a hogshead ready to send us so that we can bottle

Uncle Amédée was an avid collector of cars : De Dions, Panhards, Rocher-Schneiders, Benzes, and Pilains, even extending to Italian and American models. They were all paraded in the courtyard of Céleyran or in front of the stables at the Château du Bosc, which had been converted into garages. « They nearly always broke down and returned to their starting point pulled by two oxen, » recounted Countess Attems in her memoirs, adding that the automobile expeditions were often finished by train, several days late.

43

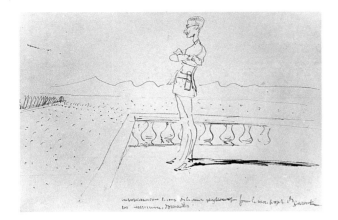

it, I've got room. I reckon that I get through a hogshead and a half each year. » Amid the general chaos of his studio, bottles from Malromé joined the pickles and foies gras, chestnut preserves and quince jellies sent by his mother : all the flavors of the southwest came to enhance his Parisian wining and dining.

SUBMERSION, *1881. The family estate at Céleyran had a vast and flourishing vineyard, which was threatened when phylloxera, the parasitic insect that attacks vine roots, invaded southern France. Vineyards were flooded in an attempt to drown the insect. Lautrec did these amusing annotated drawings of the flooded vineyards of* Céleyran when he spent the summer there. He portrayed his Uncle Amédée surveying the vines from the terraces, in the manner of a commander-in-chief supervising military operations. When, with an « Ouf! » and « Vivat! » the phylloxera was defeated, victory was celebrated in a frenzied dance watched by the figure of Lautrec below.

Lautrec is seen here sitting with his mother in the garden at Malromé in 1892. The château, situated in the Bordeaux area and possessed of a fine vineyard, was bought by Adèle de Toulouse-Lautrec in 1883. Lautrec came here every summer for a rest, before or after his holidays on the Arcachon basin. He regularly had cases or barrels of wine sent to him in Paris from Malromé.

Chapter 2

The artist's
studio :
from easel to stove

*Delectable picnics were served in the studio
and around the easel, recreating the flavors of Lautrec's
native southwest.*

« I F I had had slightly longer legs, I would never have been a painter, » confided Toulouse-Lautrec, as if to say that his art was merely a way of compensating for his deformity. In 1882 he had made his escape to Paris, equipped with the education in good food provided by the Château du Bosc and a tendency to flamboyant eccentricity exceeded only by his father's.

His parents had for ten years rented a pied-à-terre in the Hôtel Perey, rue Boissy-d'Anglas, in the Cité du Retiro close to the Royal Stables. Henri still had a few friends from his schooldays at the Lycée Fontanes in Paris, interrupted as they had been by health problems. One of these was Maurice Joyant, whom he ran into again quite by chance; when he submitted some drawings to *Paris illustré*, Lautrec found his old friend running it. The two men became inseparable. They shared a tremendous zest for life, summed up by Joyant as « a good hunger, a good thirst, and a good appreciation of food and drink. » Joined by a few friends, they formed a select group of writers, artists, scientists, and sportsmen who all loved eating well. They used to meet in restaurants — not the most fashionable, nor the most expensive, but those that most appealed to their gastronomic tastes. A prerequisite of membership of this very select circle was that indulgence of the appetite should know no limits.

While these ephemeral pleasures gave Lautrec an escape from his congenital melancholia, he at the same time applied himself to his work with enormous concentration. His remarkable talent for capturing the essence of his subject with quick pencil strokes enabled him to portray reality undisguised.

In 1882 the painter René Princeteau gave Henri advice on his handling of equestrian subjects, in which one can read the wish-fulfillment dreams of the young artist afflicted with weak legs. His drawing grew more confident in his later portrayals of the Cirque Fernando, the circus spectacle of equestriennes and trapeze artists representing a world between that of the horse and that of Paris nightlife enjoyed to the last breath.

Previous double page : Lautrec's first studio, in the heart of Montmartre, where he seriously began to develop his talent. He worked relentlessly, making forceful use of color; he detested varnish, liked chalk, pastel, and sanguine crayon; he painted on old sheets, cardboard boxes, emery cloth. The best compliment he received was from Edgar Degas, observing his use of monochrome and cinematographic composition : «Now, Lautrec, it's clear you are one of us !»

The magic stroke of Lautrec's pencil made La Goulue part of the legend of the cancan. A mercurial and insolent dancer, she fascinated Lautrec and was one of his favorite models. Others, too, became his muses, his loves, his idols, his friends, among them Rosa la Rouge, Yvette Guilbert — a singer who always wore long black gloves, and loved his company but not his painting — and Jane Avril, star of the dance halls.

Right : skirts left by models who came to pose in Lautrec's studio for ten francs a time.

In 1890 Lautrec finished AU MOULIN ROUGE, LA DANSE (DANCING AT THE MOULIN ROUGE), *one of his major works, which was hung in the entrance of the music hall. He always wore a hat when he painted «because of the light,» he said. «Lautrec's studio was so crowded with visitors on Fridays,» Gauzi recounted, «that there was nowhere to sit down; he officiated as host and kindly offered everyone a 'rainbow,' the secret of which he had told me in private.» In his shirtsleeves, a felt hat pulled down over his eyes, he prepared the cocktails behind a bar with a zinc top laden with bottles.*

He handled the shaker as skillfully as the best London barmen. Under his roof, everyone was obliged to drink, whether or not they wanted to. New arrivals were offered the « tremblement, » a curious mixture of the dregs of bottles which felled more than one of them. This initiation ceremony caused great amusement.

Adèle kept her son regularly supplied with produce from the southwest and with Malromé wine. Meals in the studio often began with foie gras and cured meats accompanied by pickled cucumbers made at the Château du Bosc. Lautrec never failed to include gastronomic reports in his letters back : « My dear mother, I can only sing hosanna on behalf of my digestion in praise of the capon, which was quite exceptional. »

that Henri first set to work in the kitchen ? Having acquired a taste for good food in childhood, he was never unwilling to share with his friends some of the secrets of his family recipes. Véfour, Ledoyen, Voisin, Riche, and other illustrious names carried on the tradition of great French cooking in Paris ; thanks to Lautrec, the habitués of Montmartre were now to discover the cooking of the Languedoc : the truffles, preserves, and foies gras that were the everyday fare of the Château du Bosc.

Lautrec lived in a succession of different places, often moving from friend to friend. When he left the Greniers, the painter Henri Rachou willingly took him in. In the midst of this peripatetic life, he would create his own secret garden, both literally and figuratively. Sometimes he set up his easel out of doors — with a very different artistic approach from that of the Impressionists ; he worked essentially in artistic isolation. Nature nonetheless provided him with an interval of calm, and the perfect background for his models. Rachou's modest garden, planted only with little trees, a few clumps of flowers, and a square of grass, was the background of several paintings. Lautrec also arranged to meet people in the nearby gardens of Père Forest, where Berthe la Sourde (Deaf Bertha) posed for him. Well shaded, and poorly frequented, although open to the public, the gardens boasted a refreshment stall and games of archery.

Henri's mother was deeply wary of the artistic circles in which he moved. She would have preferred to see him in a more conventional occupation, better suited to his social class. Though he never ceased to be loved by his family, none of them truly approved of what he did, least of all his uncle Odon who, on visiting the first exhibition of his nephew's work, wrote : « Henri paints Impressionist pictures, examples of which are on show at Goupil's, the great picture dealer. We went to see him, he will perhaps continue in the genre, which I describe as the Zola of painting. I prefer Beauty. »

But the die was cast. There was nothing to be done. Neither his mother's love nor his family's criticisms deterred Lautrec. His limping figure, his bowler hat, his little cane, had become a familiar sight in the streets of Montmartre.

Left : ÉTUDE DE NU (STUDY OF A NUDE), *1883. This is one of the first studio works done by Lautrec on his arrival in Paris. The shy, modest model, half-naked rather than nude, is an original rendering of an academic subject.*

Transparent or phosphorescent, colored with two fingers' breadth of grenadine, a dash of mint, sharpened with the juice of a lemon, or drowned in a blue lake of curaçao, the cocktail is above all a drink for social occasions.

*Previous double page :
absinthe was the
« manifesto » of the
intellectuals and artists
who regularly drank at the
Nouvelle-Athènes in the
Place Pigalle ; raised to the
ranks of an Orphic drink, it
appealed to the free and
easy. There was nothing to
equal a good « verte »
religiously served in a
stemmed glass, with water
poured drop by drop onto
the lump of sugar; it was a
passport to an « artificial
paradise. » In Lautrec's
studio, absinthe was always
on hand.*

*This Japanese warrior's
helmet, bought from an
antique dealer, was a sort
of talisman for Lautrec,
who delighted in wearing it
to fancy-dress parties
attended by his artistic and
literary friends.*

Henri de Toulouse-Lautrec-Monfa embarked on his bohemian life, with all its intrinsic difficulties : lack of money, want of a studio, absence of fixed address. In 1886 he set up a studio in the rue Caulaincourt, where he remained for over ten years. The building, every floor of which was occupied by artists, was a thoroughly bohemian place. Federico Zandomeneghi, a friend of Renoir and Manet, lived on the ground floor ; François Gauzi was up in the attic. Lautrec moved into a large room lit by bay windows on the fourth floor. If each studio reflected the character of its occupant, Lautrec's clearly showed him to be a bon viveur, fond of eating and drinking, a lover of women, essentially disorganized, a seeker after novelty, a collector of unusual and exotic objects. The one point on which he showed himself intransigent was the positioning of objects : the cleaning lady was forbidden to touch anything whatsoever. She was also forbidden to dust or sweep. Nothing, in fact, was to be cleaned, other than the area set aside for artist, model, and easel.

Apart from a ladder and an old chest, which took up a great deal of space, the furniture in the studio included a coffee table, an easel, an old sofa strewn with cushions, two straw-covered stools, and a few odd chairs. The assorted objects amounted to a collection of bric-à-brac : a dusty toy no one ever touched, two dumbbells side by side, fine Japanese vases with blue motifs, used for holding brushes, other Japanese objects such as *netsuke* and *kakemono*, and finally dancing shoes, hats from all over the world, and even a Japanese helmet. The precariously stacked books included a good range of Balzac and the Naturalist novelists of the period. The motley assembly was completed by an African spear, probably given by the explorer Ballay on his return from a trip to the Congo, the usual crate of food sent regularly from Rouergue, and, on the wall, a painted parody of *Le Bois sacré cher aux arts et aux muses*. This canvas was a criticism of Pierre Puvis de Chavannes's award-winning work exhibited at the Salon of 1884. The parody was completed in two days by Cormon's pupils and signed by Lautrec on behalf of them all. It survived as a souvenir of an art student's prank, and features Henri himself, his back turned, his rear view presented to the Muses.

Henri collected albums of Japanese prints, mostly erotic, which he kept in a drawer. Like the Impressionists, he was influenced by *ukiyo-e*, an art at once delicate and boldly colored. From the Land of the Rising Sun, he obtained the traditional flat box containing Indian ink, brushes, and fixative, doubtless ordered through Samuel Bing, a fashionable aesthete whose Paris gallery exhibited Japanese art. When Maurice Joyant took over the Goupil gallery on the death of Theo van Gogh, he commissioned Lautrec to put this marvelous collection of prints in order. The landscapes of Hokusai and Hiroshige, and Utamaro's brothel scenes, held an endless fascination for him.

The objects in Lautrec's studio were in a constant state of flux, disappearing only to be replaced immediately by something else acquired on the artist's frequent nocturnal escapades and travels, such as the Liberty print brought back from his first trip to London, which displaced the hanging from Karaman. He never parted, however, with his reproductions of Uccello's *Battle of San Romano* and Carpaccio's *Courtesans Playing with Animals*, his constant points of reference in the history of art. This miscellaneous collection of objects revealed his eclectic tastes.

Pictures in the studio were stacked face to the wall in rows ; portfolios of drawings lay scattered on the floor. From time to time, Lautrec received representatives of the art world, collectors, and the occasional dealer. Among them was Arsène Alexandre, one of the rare critics — possibly the only one — interested in his work from the outset, and the only one to follow his career to the end. « In the miserable ordeal from which I am emerging, Alexandre has proved the most loyal and best of friends and has put everything to rights, » wrote the artist after a period in a psychiatric asylum. An article by Alexandre, published in *Le Figaro* on March 30, 1889, under the title « Une guérison » (« A Cure »), explained the artist's condition in terms both sympathetic and realistic.

The studio was always open to models and friends, who would gather around whatever dish the artist felt inspired to prepare that day. Vincent van Gogh was a discreet but frequent visitor. Disinclined to conversation, his latest painting tucked under his arm, he came

61

LE REPOS DU MODÈLE
(MODEL RESTING), *1889.*
Lautrec painted young
ladies «who had only their
blouse to separate them
from their profession.»
Fascinated by the voluptuous
pallor of a relaxed body, the
shadow of the nape of the
neck, the light on a protruding
collarbone, «Lautrec never
stopped looking at his
model... If he had a desire
to touch her, it was the
desire of living flesh passing
into his hands and making
them tremble. To inspire
him to work, he needed a
woman he could see was
alive» (Thadée Natanson).

Right : in the 1890s
American bars sprang up
here and there in Paris.
The first cocktail recipes in
French were published by
Alphonse Allais in 1902 in
Captain Cap. *It is likely*
that the witty «Alphy» and
the no less ironical Lautrec,
who both worked on the
Revue blanche, *exchanged*
a few recipes.

to meet the Lautrec « clan, » colleagues from his days in the Cormon studio : Gauzi, Rachou, Grenier. He followed the conversation, observed the others present, examined Lautrec's latest works, then took his place on a stool in the corner, eventually leaving as silently as he had arrived ; his own painting passed unnoticed.

For ordinary professional dealings and sales, the studio was open on Fridays, by appointment only. Visitors were obliged to fall in with Lautrec's ideas, which he enshrined as rules of conduct not to be transgressed : « Properly to appreciate a painting, » he would say, « one has to drink a good cocktail first. » The next step was inevitable : before any discussion was possible, he headed for a table laden with a multicolored range of bottles, as well stocked as the Café Weber, from which he had « pinched » the secret of the « rainbow » cocktail. He stocked the best brands of whisky, gin, Armagnac, brandy, and port, and, when funds allowed, vintage champagne. A skillful barman, well versed in the new art of the cocktail, he delighted in concocting daring mixtures with a great variety of alcohols : Byrrh, vermouth, maraschino, chartreuse, curaçao, and the inevitable bottle of absinthe, the favored poison of up-to-date people. He got hold of a set of silver goblets in which to mix his drinks, and always carried on his person a little nutmeg grater, sprinkling the spice on port to bring out its bouquet. He flavored a number of desserts with nutmeg and added it even to foie gras.

No friendship worthy of the name went unpledged by a drink, made as pleasing to the eye as to the palate. Lautrec served the cocktails in a random collection of glasses, mostly picked up on his nightly drinking rounds, and would only allow conversation to begin once some explosive mixture had been swallowed. He refused to divulge its ingredients, which at times proved as undrinkable as they were intoxicating. From the barman of the Austin Bar he had obtained the recipe for a « corpse reviver, » fit only for stomachs lined with steel. The preparation of this cocktail of unimaginable alcoholic strength required patience and deftness. It involved pouring twelve liqueurs of different colors over a little spoon, taking infinite care not to mix them. « Tek-Nik, » Lautrec boasted in triumph as everyone marveled at his rainbow drink.

The zest for life that infused Lautrec's art also found expression in his entertaining and cooking, setting the pace of daily life in the studio. His hospitality was not, however, indiscriminate : his highly prized dish of young wood pigeon with olives, for example, he served only to connoisseurs. Anyone he thought pretentious or snobbish, or suspected of wanting to sample the « Lautrec specialty » out of curiosity alone, he would unceremoniously turn away, giving as his reason : « They are not worthy of the 'pigeon aux olives,' they will never have it, they will never know what it is. » This recipe, perfected for his most discerning friends, seemed to him to reach the heights of culinary excellence. A gleam of relish shone in his eyes as he presided over the serving of the plump birds, golden brown, aromatic, tender, accompanied by a sauceboat of steaming hot gravy. This was the masterpiece of the artist-cook, who would happily entertain a maximum of eight to ten guests at his table — not necessarily all from the art world.

When it came to laying the table, Lautrec was punctilious. The linen and silver came from his family. There were no useless ornaments on the table, other than little bunches of flowers and carafes of water in which goldfish were swimming — a decorative touch that had a point to make : in Lautrec's opinion, to drink water was to insult one's palate and ruin one's appreciation of good food. He was liable to react angrily if anyone dared commit this iconoclastic deed. Nothing could rival a *grand cru*, or so loosen the tongues of wine lovers.

His cooking was a personal and somewhat curious blend of family recipes from southwest France and others acquired in the course of his travels. At the stove Lautrec gave free rein to his inventiveness, preparing for his guests exciting dishes accompanied by colorful, highly seasoned sauces, and not hesitating on occasion to double the proportions of certain ingredients. Like the ancients, Lautrec considered garlic indispensable : it enhanced the humblest crouton, the flavor of sauces and meats. He devised his own method of extracting the medicinal properties of the bulb by marinating the cloves not in oil but in port, and recommended that this « magic » potion be drunk at bedtime. For

« Would you be able to give me six small tablecloths, a few table napkins... A few very ordinary table knives would be equally useful. In short I am getting married without a wife, » Lautrec wrote to his mother. The studio provided the setting for his dinner parties, which revealed the taste for good living acquired in his childhood. Jane Avril sometimes acted as hostess on these occasions.

Right : «*I like people who have a cannibalistic streak in them and say when they come for lunch : 'I am hungry.'»* To such appreciative souls Lautrec would serve scallops accompanied by onions stuffed with garlic purée and spiked with cloves. This recipe, given the name «onions à la Toulouse-Lautrec,» was the painter's own adaptation of a dish originally offered to him by Alfred Edwards, Misia Natanson's second husband. It satisfied his taste for seasoning and spice.

64

lery and shop, the Salon de l'Art Nouveau, rue de Provence. Here he exhibited the work of this group of innovatory artists, including glass by René Lalique and Emile Gallé, stained glass by Tiffany, furniture by Henry van de Velde.

The buffet served by Lautrec suggested a childrens' party : there were little saucers of curds, Fontainebleau cheeses wrapped in muslin, fluffy Chantilly cream, carafes of milk, and whipped cream cheese. A few bright touches of color were provided by dishes of red fruit and wreaths of wild flowers. This frugal picnic was left to the ladies. The host had not forgotten the drinkers. Tucked away in a corner, a barman dressed in white busied himself with a cocktail shaker. He prepared « alexandras, » milkshakes sprinkled with nutmeg, a « pousse-l'amour » — an exotic mixture of maraschino, crème vanille verte, and Cognac bound with an egg yolk. Lautrec himself mixed « corpse revivers » and « maiden blushes, » and could not resist improvising a few explosive cocktails. « Everyone enjoyed themselves drinking, laughing, playing the flute, rolling up their invitations, lithographs on which a fine cow represented the beauty of summer, » concluded the account in the *Vie parisienne.*

Left : SELF-PORTRAIT, *1882-83. Studious and determined, a touch nostalgic too, this contrasts with Lautrec's ironic and humorous caricatures of himself. This was the period in which Lautrec first discovered Montmartre, a district with a somewhat dubious reputation, popular with artists, full of little gardens and unassuming houses.*

Exhausted by alcohol, sleepless nights, and work in his studio, Lautrec was able to fall asleep anywhere : even in front of the Prince of Wales, future Edward VII of England, who opened his exhibition in London. Lautrec would often fall asleep in the carriage that took him home at night. When the driver, noticing his failure to get out, ventured to wake him, the furious Lautrec would tell him « to mind his own business » and go on peacefully sleeping in the stationary vehicle outside his front door.

Chapter 3

Bachelor friendship

*At male dinners, at large social gatherings,
at tête-à-tête suppers, at gourmet weekends
with friends, every meal was a party,
every dish a treat.*

WHILE Toulouse-Lautrec could be perfectly agreeable, even delightful, he was just as liable to be grumpy, irascible, indeed intolerable in his behavior — perhaps his way of venting the frustrations he suffered. There were also times when he was authoritarian and capricious, requiring everyone to be at his beck and call.

His first cousin, Gabriel Tapié de Céleyran, who was five years his junior, had come to Paris to further his medical studies and was often cast in the role of Lautrec's whipping boy. « The doctor, » as Gabriel was known, would suffer his tyrannical behavior in silence. Paul Leclerq, a close friend, remembered how the painter « turned red with rage » on seeing Gabriel shake hands with someone whose face displeased him.

The doctor's long-suffering patience was matched only by his admiration for the artist. The relationship between the two men was touching — sometimes sarcastic on Henri's part, but always affectionate. He loved to tease Gabriel, calling him all sorts of names, from « rascally tapir » to « Ceylonese rabbit. » His worst insult, when the doctor uttered an opinion to which he objected, was to enunciate the word « in-ca-pa-ble, » syllable by syllable. The cousins were inseparable, going together to shows, to the races, to cafés-concerts, to restaurants, to Parisian dinners. One could hardly run into the little man leaning on his tiny stick without catching sight, a pace or two away, of the sloping shoulders of Cousin Gabriel, silent and gangling, but always meticulously turned out.

« Don't bother about that, Charlotte. » This was a favorite expression of Lautrec's, and he used it to put the doctor in his place when the latter ventured to remark that one should not cook in one's host's drawing room. Invited to dine by Georges-Henri Manuel in the company of a few relations, Lautrec had offered to cook lobster à l'américaine. The dinner in question was held in a luxurious apartment in the rue François Premier, inhabited by an obsessive bachelor with a passion for good furniture and fine objects. Nothing would make

Previous double page : «He loved to talk about cooking and had a number of unusual recipes for the most everyday ingredients. Toulouse-Lautrec cooked as well as he ate.... The preparation of a lobster à l'américaine held no secrets for him, » recounted one of his friends, the Symbolist poet Paul Leclerq.

Portrait of Toulouse-Lautrec staying with the Natansons at Villeneuve-sur-Yonne, painted in 1898 by Édouard Vuillard. The

portrait recalls one of the many visits Vuillard and Lautrec paid to the Natansons. Gastronomy featured large in this country house, where friendships were forged around the dining-room table.

Above : GABRIEL TAPIÉ DE CÉLEYRAN. *This tall, lanky figure was fascinated by the turbulent genius of his cousin Henri, who portrayed him in mischievous caricatures. Gabriel's admiration for his cousin was boundless, and the two men were inseparable companions.*

The dining room of Lautrec's friend Georges-Henri Manuel, a meticulous character who loved art, was typical of the world of the Parisian bourgeoisie, with its all-pervading scent of polished wood. Furnished with huge green plants, dark paneling, mirrors, and pictures up to the ceiling, it provided the setting for memorable bachelor dinners.

Previous double page : a gourmet and an inspired chef, Lautrec tackled cooking with the same astonishing verve that fueled his artistic work and made him one of the most colorful figures of the late nineteenth century. Invited by a friend to cook a lobster à l'américaine in his flat, he refused to work in the kitchen, and staged a spectacular culinary performance in the drawing room, which was hastily covered with sheets to protect the furniture.

Above and right : decorative touches are provided by the dish of fruit and the floral arrangement accompanying the zabaglione.

our stubborn cook change his mind : he refused outright to go to the kitchen, determined that his fellow guests should witness the preparation of the meal. After all, does it not increase one's pleasure to enjoy the spectacle of food being prepared, before gratifying the stomach where, according to Rivarol, « the roots of the spirit grow » ?

A little stove, saucepans, and all the necessary ingredients were brought to the drawing room under the watchful eye of the host, who was anxious about his furniture, which had been hastily covered in sheets and cloths. In this improvised setting the cook set to work, enveloped in a white apron that was much too long for him ; he cooked with feverish concentration, generating a tremendous feeling of suspense. In no time at all exquisite smells pervaded the room ; then came the magic moment when the dish was set aflame, without any damage being done to the furniture. The results could now be enjoyed with relish, having been prepared according to the finest principles of cooking.

Had Lautrec ever written a cookbook, the chapters devoted to shellfish and game would undoubtedly have predominated. Lobster, referred to in contemporary culinary works as « the cardinal of the sea, » was his favorite seafood. The markets of Les Halles, in Paris, were very well supplied, ocean produce being delivered quickly by railroad while still alive. But however fresh the shellfish, in Lautrec's eyes nothing was ever quite equal to that found at the seaside in the hollows of the rocks. Fish and shellfish brought back memories of holidays on the Atlantic, where he went to restore his health, far from the cabarets and nightlife of Montmartre. He consumed them in quantity on weekend trips to the Normandy coast and during summer holidays in southwest France, divided between his mother's château in Bordeaux and the coast of Taussat in the Arcachon basin.

Lautrec preferred the slow pace of the steamer to the fast but « shaking » progress of the locomotive. This method of transport gave him the illusion of setting off to distant lands like Japan, a journey he planned but never realized. A cargo boat used to set out from Le Havre for Africa, skirting the Atlantic coast, calling at Bordeaux, then at Lisbon, before arriving in Dakar.

A TABLE CHEZ M. ET Mme NATANSON (AT TABLE, CHEZ M. AND Mme NATANSON), *1895, shows one of the many gatherings of friends organized by the couple. The social columns extolled Misia's goddesslike mien, her magnificient clothes, her marvelous style of entertaining. The Egeria of the* Revue blanche *was a leader of fashion and always chose her company «following the dictates of her heart.» In Lautrec's painting, the Swiss artist*

Félix Vallotton is recognizable on her left and Vuillard on her right.

Right : at the Natanson's party, solid cocktails were served : Ostend oysters sprinkled with cayenne pepper, drowned in alcohol, and then set alight.

furniture and turned into the « Bar des Alexandre. » In front of a long mahogany counter were a few high stools, on which drinkers could comfortably perch. A notice, between two liqueur advertisements, warned : « Don't speak to the man at the wheel, » in other words, the barman. Impassive, silent, virtually unrecognizable, with head and beard shaved, apart from two comically tiny patches, Lautrec was dressed in a white jacket and a waistcoat made out of the American flag. His assistant was, in an amusing juxtaposition, Maxime Dethomas, a colossus nearly 6 1/2 feet tall, dressed similarly in white.

Some three hundred guests, the cream of Paris society, watched the maneuvers of these two astonishing waiters, juggling their flasks and shakers. A complete list of the drinks on offer would defy belief : champagne, port, apéritif wines flavored with quinquina, Lillet — a new drink made not far from Malromé — syrups, eaux-de-vie, Cognac, Armagnac, Calvados, whisky, gin... Everything Lautrec could think of was to be found there. Nor did he omit the customary cocktail snacks, hot sauces, and spices, without which everything tasted bland : Worcester sauce, cloves, nutmeg, paprika, red pepper, not to mention bitters, extracted from the bark of the shrub called angostura.

The evening began promisingly, launched with a few innovatory drinks, mild and sparkling at first, increasingly robust and alcoholic. Lethal concoctions followed, setting a few unwary throats on fire : « solid » cocktails, such as oysters with cayenne pepper, and sardines in gin flambé in port. A range of drinks to be downed in a single gulp was succeeded by a series of delicately flavored pink cocktails, best sipped through a straw.

Known for his strong head, Alfred Jarry was nonetheless among the first to collapse onto a sofa, closely followed by Félix Fénéon. Jules Renard, who sat at a small table with his wife, surveyed the battlefield and amused himself by counting the victims. Arriving late, cold and famished from a bicycle trip on the outskirts of Paris, Vuillard and Bonnard were unable to withstand the diabolical concoctions. Inebriated, like so many before them, they collapsed into the arms of the

Left : LA REVUE BLANCHE, *1895. The party given by Alexandre Natanson and his brother Thadée, founder of* La Revue blanche, *was a memorable occasion. The most scintillating members of Paris society gathered around Thadée's wife Misia, muse of the artistic avant-garde. She enchanted Lautrec, who used her as the model for one of the covers he designed for* La Revue blanche.

Lemons, an essential ingredient in some of the cocktails, are here transformed into little pigs by Lautrec's imagination. The evening was brought to an end with a few lines addressed to the barman by Romain Coolus : «Ah, Toulouse-Lautrec, I can see that you are envied as a barman for your astonishing Grecian profile. »

97

SUZANNE VALADON,
1886-1887. She was an
equestrienne before she met
Lautrec and turned to
painting. Suzanne was his
mistress, until he realized
that she was calculatedly
looking for a husband. His
models often wore a hat,
an accessory that delighted
him as much as a black
glove on a slender hand.

Right : Lautrec applied no
hierarchy to his pleasures.
There was sensual delight
to be taken in the female
figure, and also in a dish
of slowly roasted lamb.

housemaids and English governesses who acted as nurses for the evening. All that Vuillard could afterward remember of the occasion was waking up, fully dressed, shoes still on his feet, in his hostess's bed when she came to her room in the early hours of the morning.

Some managed, despite their drunken state, to keep their dignity, but others walked straight into the trap laid by the satanic Lautrec, who, for once, had not touched a single drop of alcohol. He surveyed the proceedings out of a corner of his eye, and performed his duties with the utmost seriousness. Later, he was to boast of having served more than two thousand glasses that evening. The next day the Paris gossip columnists talked of nothing but the exorbitant cost of the party, and rumor duly turned the singular and hilarious occasion into a Roman orgy.

It is true to say that for Lautrec a meal was insipid if not spiced up with a bit of fun. His capacity for extravagant and whimsical behavior was limitless, and disturbing to people who did not know him well enough to understand the impulsive and ironical streak in his character. He was amused by everything, including other people's astonishment. When he went to the Nouveau Cirque, the sight of a kangaroo boxing with a man gave him the idea for a gastronomic practical joke. Remembering that nothing could match the flavor of kangaroo meat, he invited a few of his friends to eat it. As the marsupial was unobtainable in Paris, he substituted a sheep from Ouessant, having asked his butcher to sew the tail of a cow onto it. The sauce, which combined foie gras, truffles in abundance, bolets, chanterelle and morel mushrooms, was thinned with three bottles of Chambertin and a good dose of 1811 champagne. It accompanied the roast, generously larded, stuffed with basil and wild thyme, and cooked for several hours. After all the preparation, the animal was presented in a little apron, from which there escaped a white mouse, mischievously slipped in by Lautrec.

Lautrec's meals were said to arouse a sense of breathtaking suspense in his guests : anything could happen in the hands of this defier of convention. After one particular banquet, at which wine flowed with its customary freedom, they were left waiting for dessert. Promising delicious sweetmeats, their host con-

ducted them, to their surprise, to a modest apartment inhabited by the Dihaus, musicians and friends. « Here is your dessert ! » he said, in front of a painting by Degas : a portrait of Désiré Dihau playing the bassoon in the orchestra of the Opéra.

Nothing gave Lautrec greater satisfaction than startling and provoking others. It seemed to be his daily revenge against an obstructive fate. His pronounced partiality for jokes was indulged by his female friends. Suzanne Valadon was happy to play her part. An equestrienne, for a period, in the Cirque Molier, she was noticed by Puvis de Chavannes and became his mistress and his model before turning to painting in her own right, and meeting Lautrec. They had a passionate and stormy relationship, interspersed by infidelities, and broken off after she feigned a suicide attempt.

For one of his dinners alone with her, Lautrec got Léontine to prepare a succulent leg of lamb. It was cooked for seven hours, making it almost melt in the mouth. The pickled vegetable accompanying the dish followed a recipe whispered in his ear by Madame Blanche, a masseuse in Montmartre. After a while the meal began to seem interminable. Lautrec's response was to enliven the dessert at the cook's expense. « Undress, » he ordered, « so that we can see Léontine's face ! » Suzanne Valadon fell in with his wishes. She unfastened her skirt, took off her frilly blouse, and slipped off her petticoat and corset, leaving on only her stockings and ankle boots. Lautrec could now ring for Léontine. After a somewhat surprised start, she imperturbably served the dessert. But the next day she made a shocked complaint to Bourges, who threatened to tell Lautrec's mother of his extravagant behavior.

Left : according to Grimod de La Reynière, love and gastronomic pleasures are not particularly compatible, and the best table companions were not necessarily the best lovers. « What became of the beautiful blonde girl you used only to eat with ? » Jean-Louis Forain once asked his friend Lautrec.

Foie gras and lamb cooked for seven hours paved the way for seduction. Lautrec's taste in food tended to the robust. Provincial and full of flavor, it showed his attachment to his family roots ; aromatic and highly seasoned, with spices and condiments both regional and exotic, it revealed his delight in innovation.

101

The delicate scent of flowers and intimate lighting set the scene for a tête-à-tête dinner in the comfortable apartment Lautrec shared with his friend Doctor Bourges.

Silversmiths and glassmakers designed these long-necked flower vases. It was fashionable for stems to lean, spill over, and intertwine following the dictates of Art Nouveau.

Right : a leg of lamb, still succulent after seven hours of cooking, and so tender that it could supposedly be eaten with a spoon.

Following pages : the sinfully delicious « serpent du couvent » (« convent snake ») is served on a bed of angelica and crystallized fruits. The presentation of a dish and the arrangement of the table were very important to Lautrec, whose artistic sensibility and appreciation of color also found expression in his culinary interest.

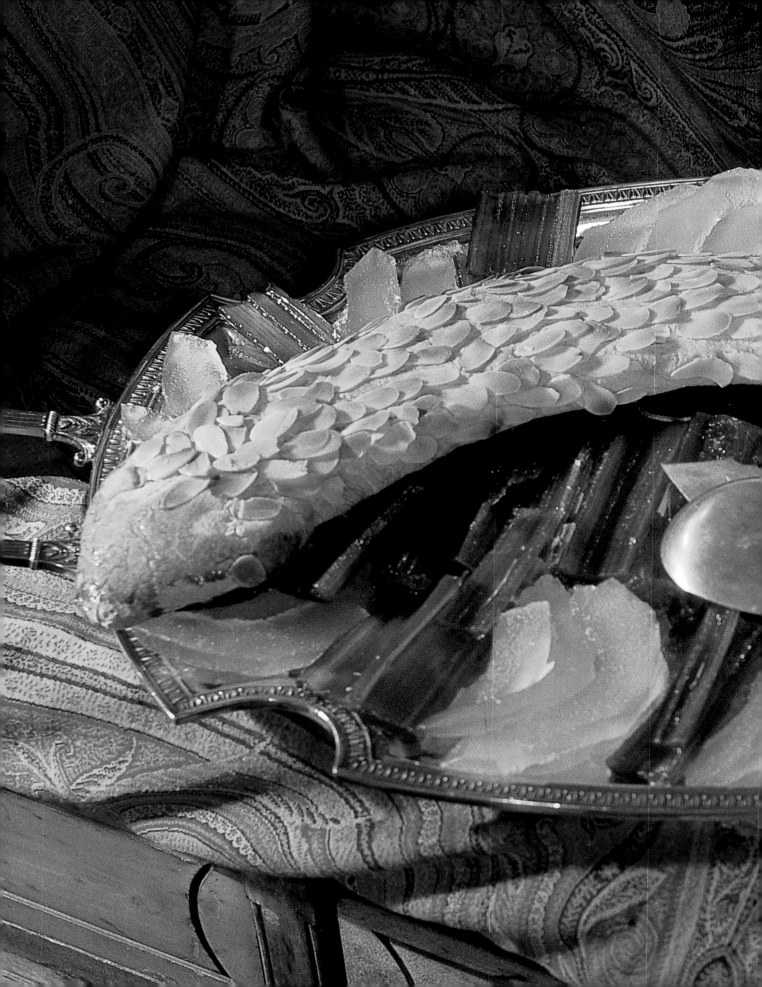

Chapter 4

The round of pleasure : from brothel to café-concert

*The world of an epicurean painter, a singular
little man with a mad passion for dance, noise,
the good life, and the female sex.*

« I AM camping in a brothel, » he explained casually, as if it were the most natural thing in the world, to friends worried by his disappearances for days at a time. Notwithstanding the large number on the façade of the building, and its red light, the address that was known to every man was kept a secret. The brothel was part of a man's private life. There the adolescent lost his virginity, the bachelor came briefly to escape his loneliness, the married man to relieve the monotony of his conjugal bed. The parlor, with its pearly lampshades, was to its visitors — and how numerous they were — a type of very private club. In this exotic oasis, shut away behind shutters that never opened and heavy dark-red drapes, men tossed back champagne before enacting their fantasies. Lautrec chose to live there. The « girls » surrounded him with every imaginable attention, and knew when to keep out of the way. He once made an appointment in a brothel with the well-known — and very serious — picture dealer Paul Durand-Ruel, who wanted to look at his work. The latter apparently noticed nothing untoward, taking the place to be the artist's private home.

It is indeed astonishing that this aristocrat should have received his friends in such a place — and led astray a number of bachelors in his circle, such as Romain Coolus, Maurice Guibert, and Maxime Dethomas, whom he invited to the madam's table. However, our priapic jester felt quite at home in the peculiarly self-contained world of the brothel, and at establishments such as Lesbos à La Souris, run by Madame Palmyre with her dog Bouboule.

The streetwalkers of the rue d'Amboise were on affectionate and friendly terms with Lautrec, and remained curiously untouched and undisturbed by the life they led. They were simple working girls of easy virtue, seeking, whether from loneliness or a broken heart or financial necessity, a way out of their lot. Lautrec shared their daily lives, partook of their most intimate moments, and immortalized them on his canvases, without cruelty, and also without illusion. Beau-

Previous double page : in the brothels Lautrec experienced an intimacy that was lacking in the rest of his life. « It was said that Lautrec, unhappy in love, went to the brothel in search of comfort and also images for his art. His primary interest was to observe or to obtain satisfaction. When it was not, as everywhere else, to drink » (Thadée Natanson).

FEMME TIRANT SON BAS (WOMAN ADJUSTING HER STOCKING), *1894. An everyday scene in a brothel, painted from life : dressing in preparation for a customer. The girls attired themselves in tunics slit open to the thigh, and silk gowns allowing a glimpse of suspenders and black stockings, pulled straight.*

The inmates of the brothel in the rue Amboise. An establishment was judged by the quality of the women it offered. The prostitutes, of different types, were supposed to create the charm of the place and satisfy their customers's tastes.

Right : an Oriental lamp, casting its exotic light on the activities of the brothel.

Left : Lautrec shared the
life of the prostitutes in the
rue des Moulins behind its
wall of thick hangings.
More than a customer, he
was a friend, confidant,
and regular visitor. He once
acted as host there to the
highly respectable Paul
Durand-Ruel, Claude
Monet's patron and dealer.
This gifted man, who
closely followed the latest
artistic developments and
was capable of buying
dozens of paintings at one
time, took an interest in
Lautrec's work.

LES DEUX AMIES (THE TWO
FRIENDS), *1895.
Exchanging confidences,
with little kisses, caresses,
and tokens of affection, two
prostitutes relax in bed. The
communal life of the
brothel made them
intimate : they shared
everything, including
customers, and often spent
the night together.
« Whatever... set the girls in
the brothel gossiping, or
made them laugh or cry,
interested [Lautrec] as much
as any social chitchat or
happening at dinner parties
in town » (Thadée
Natanson).*

tiful or ugly, young or decrepit, utterly naïve or blatantly depraved, they provided him with a kaleidoscopic array of the careless gestures, the inner secrets, of twenty-four hours in the life of a prostitute. He was addressed as Monsieur Henri, and his visits caused no surprise. His arrival was heralded by the tapping of his stick on the steps of the staircase up to the second floor. Then, going down the passages, he would start singing the *Chant du départ* : « La République nous appelle... La République nous attend... » (« The Republic calls us... The Republic awaits us... »).

The prevailing atmosphere in the rue d'Amboise was strangely respectable. The madam was a strong character, who made sure that the girls behaved properly ; she settled any problems and kept everything in good decorative order. The least one could do was to offer visitors a little sexual relaxation. And given the infinite variety of brothels, it was important to establish a good reputation.

When the time came to redecorate the main reception room, the madam turned to Lautrec, stipulating the one condition that he preserve the existing air of respectability. Neither the girls in the brothel nor the clients would have understood anything else. The current artistic fashion was for inspirational scenes on more or less mythological subjects, and Lautrec was well acquainted with the prissy period taste for academic paintings of Venus, smooth as almond paste, and of Leda, enveloped in whipped cream. He was amused by the prospect of becoming a « painter-of-all-works, » and started to put together large pictures, each including a medallion of a woman's head and decorated with rococo motifs, canopies, roses, and climbing flowers inspired by documents published by the Goupil gallery. The pernickety and repetitive nature of the task bored him, however, and, shortly after embarking on it, he called on a number of friends to help, among them Puvis de Chavannes and a local housepainter. The goddesses gave place to the inmates of the brothel, whose portraits Lautrec painted on a straw-colored background.

Of all the women who were his models, and sometimes his friends, Lautrec preferred Mireille, a faded blonde with extravagant makeup whom he had met in the brothel of the rue des Moulins. She was still young, already disillusioned. His attraction to the girl was quickly spotted by the madam, who would spirit her away whenever Lautrec was expected. By giving the brothel keeper a little money, he managed to take Mireille out for a while. She came to his studio to pose, and he gave her bouquets of violets. She is the principal figure, seated in the foreground, of *Dans le salon : rue des Moulins (In the Salon : Rue des Moulins)*, painted in 1894.

In the hierarchy of brothels, the rue des Moulins was a cozy, luxurious, sexual « house of dreams, » tucked away from the commotion of Paris. Lautrec was received there by silent maids in starched white aprons. The great cut-glass mirrors in the large reception room reflected its furnishings, soft divans, sofas covered in purple velvet, Turkish artifacts, little occasional tables inlaid with mother-of-pearl. Kentias, luxuriant plants with large palmate leaves, very popular in English interiors, gave the room the atmosphere of a greenhouse.

In the bedrooms nothing detracted from the effect of easy sensuality. Oriental materials, ottomans, animal skins, and the scent of patchouli excited the male imagination. Clients with a taste for the exotic chose the Japanese or Moorish rooms, while the more conventional opted for the neo-Gothic or Pompadour styles.

When one reached the back of the house, a smell of caramelized apple tart wafted out of the pantry. Surprising as it might seem, life in a brothel had many parallels with life in a boarding school. The girls were subject to strict discipline and supervision of their daily lives. They slept in dormitories and ate in a refectory. In the rest period they knitted, hummed the odd sentimental tune, and exchanged confidences, while the more superstitious of them read cards. They dressed themselves up, put on makeup, and hung around the drawing room waiting for a client. If one of them married, Lautrec was the first to be informed by a joint card, identified by the briefest possible address : « The ladies, rue des Moulins. » « Isn't that splendid, eh ! » he would say in amusement to his friends.

How did Lautrec manage to indulge the pleasures of the flesh without relinquishing the pleasures of the

DÉBAUCHE, *1896. An intimate scene in a brothel. The girls, sprawled on the divans, in an alcoholic haze, were a constant source of inspiration to Lautrec. «One could see him completely lost in the depths of a bosom, purring with pleasure. Another time he wrapped two vast breasts round his neck, like a living scarf» (Thadée Natanson). Solicitous of the welfare of his friends, he took Romain Coolus and Maurice Guibert (portrayed here) to Paris-Cythère.*

Following pages : the Japanese room, luxurious, soft, and delicately colored. Some afternoons the girls played cards with Lautrec, who never forgot to give them a present for their birthdays. He chose boxes of irresistible delicacies from Giraudin, beautifully presented and quickly emptied, or souvenirs, such as a scarf bought at the Universal Exposition of 1889. «They learned from him something wholly new to them : consideration» (Thadée Natanson).

In constrast to the rooms open to customers, the dining room was simple, minimally furnished with wooden tables and rustic benches, on which the girls gathered at fixed mealtimes.

Left : a refreshing salad of lamb's lettuce with truffles, which were sent to Lautrec from southwest France.

CES DAMES AU RÉFECTOIRE (THOSE WOMEN IN THE DINING ROOM), *1893-94. In well-run brothels the food was good, as a way of keeping the girls. They all came down to the dining room at about 7 P.M. for the second meal of the day, the longest and most copious, presided over by the madam, or Lautrec when he was there.*

Everyday tableware of the period was decorated with satirical subjects, La Fontaine's fables, historical events, or pictorial puzzles.

Right : the simplest of desserts was also one of the best — pears cooked in wine flavored with a few cloves and grains of black pepper.

table ? His escapades in brothels were very carefully organized. He first packed his bags and shut up his studio, leaving behind neither his drawing pencils nor his sketchbooks, nor indeed the terrines of foie gras from his native southwest, the truffles vital to his cooking, the bottles of Sauternes and Léoville-Barton so pleasing to his palate. Sometimes he would himself set to work at the stove, searching out the recipe for tripe with saffron from his native region, a dish prepared by the servants at the Château du Bosc, and better known in the locality as *tripoux de Naucelle*. Alternatively he might use a recipe brought back from one of his trips to England, Belgium, or Spain. He recounted, for example, how the recipe for Spanish rice — a la Valenciana — had been given to him by a flamenco dancer whom he met in Madrid. Friendships were forged at these gatherings around the table in the brothel. The rest of the time the attentive madam, in the role of experienced housewife, would satisfy Monsieur Henri's culinary appetites, preparing a capon on a bed of truffles, or a chicken in dry white wine. She would always reserve his favorite morsel for him, the oysters of the fowl.

What would have become of the nights of Montmartre without Lautrec, who, playing the part of voyeur, so brilliantly portrayed the district's « midnight civilization » ? And what would have become of Lautrec, who detested solitude above all else, without his panoply of friends ? Without the serried characters who, through the medium of his art, came to embody a style.

Lautrec took to frequenting the Nouvelle-Athènes, a literary café on a corner of the Place Pigalle, popular with the Impressionists and pupils in Cormon's studio, young art students who wore long, wide ties known as *lavallières*. A place was kept for him there in the evenings, the hour for absinthe. This drink, which Charles Baudelaire called the « artificial ideal » and Jean Lorrain the « wandering vice, » which Paul Verlaine elevated to the realms of poetry by describing it as the « green fairy, » measured no less than sixty-two degrees alcohol. But, more than a vice, much more than the fashionable drug of the elite and snobbish, this scourge of the artists of Montmartre and the writers of Montparnasse was, at the beginning of the

When he finished *Dancing at the Moulin Rouge* in 1890, they bought the painting and hung it in the entrance hall. Some of the Moulin's regular visitors appear in the work — Lautrec liked to portray friends and acquaintances, and indeed himself, among the audience. The thirty or so pictures he made of the establishment are in effect secret snapshots of its nightlife.

Artistic realism was not, however, without its dangers, as Lautrec was to discover when Zidler gave him permission to exhibit his paintings in a wide corridor leading to the dance hall. One of these pictures portrayed La Goulue with a friend and Môme Fromage. All that is shown of the unlovely friend is a corner of an eye, her chignon, and her shoulder... but it was enough to make the girls at the Moulin recognize her and explode with laughter. The unfortunate object of their mirth was furious and a tremendous row ensued. In high dudgeon, La Goulue threatened to leave the Moulin if the picture responsible for all the trouble were not immediately taken down. Lautrec's poster, commissioned by Zidler to advertise the new show in 1891, fortunately met with a better reception.

« There is nothing to beat the poster, » Lautrec confided one day to his cousin, with his characteristic way of swallowing his syllables, as they were looking at advertisements for France Champagne by Bonnard and for the Moulin Rouge by Gustave Chéret. Lautrec had both of these on display in his studio, and he was longing to try his hand at lithography, never having had the opportunity. Chéret was the undoubted master of the large advertisement at that time. Described by Manet as « the Watteau of the streets, » he was first to have the brilliant idea of featuring attractive stereotyped women on advertising posters. They soon took over the boulevard Haussmann. Lautrec's poster, which portrayed La Goulue in a revolutionary cinematographic manner, momentarily eclipsed the more anodyne « darlings » on view elsewhere.

She is pictured in a red blouse with white spots, her chignon perched high on her head, dancing in front of a row of dark silhouettes representing the audience. The poster met with universal public acclaim, while the critics launched into discussion of its lines, arabesques, and monochrome areas of Japanese in-

Left : André Antoine at the Théâtre Libre and Aurélien Lugné-Poe at the Théâtre de l'Œuvre commissioned contemporary artists to design their programs and posters. Lautrec was involved in the 1893-94 season. He portrayed Sarah Bernhardt in the role of Phèdre and Réjane in that of Madame Sans-Gêne. In 1895 he designed the set for Victor Barrucand's Chariot en terre cuite at the Théâtre de l'Œuvre, and the following year collaborated with Bonnard and Vuillard on the set of Ubu Roi.

When he went to the theater, Lautrec replaced his bowler hat with a top hat and put on a suit. He often went to the Comédie-Française with his cousin Gabriel Tapié de Céleyran, and loved its atmosphere, its characteristic smell, the dark-red velvet of the seats, the foyer, and the well-bred usherettes in their caps.

Following page :
LA CLOWNESSE ASSISE
(Cha-U-Kao), 1896.

127

spiration. La Goulue, who had no interest in art, remained indifferent to all the « intellectual jargon, » preferring to consider Lautrec as « her » official painter. True to this role, he later decorated the booth in which she performed at a fairground, by then a faded but « unique star. »

Paris at the period offered a magnificent display of posters. Not a stretch of wall, not a blank façade, went unadorned. And special little carts bearing advertisements were wheeled up and down the great boulevards through the crowds. Encouraged by Maurice Joyant and advised by Bonnard, Lautrec plunged into poster design. A meticulous technician, he inspected every proof, fixing on the most minor detail, decided which were to be kept, which rejected. Over three hundred lithographs were thus produced, most of them portraits, and roughly thirty posters. Some, however, failing to meet the approval of the customer, proved but a limited success, if not actually controversial. Lautrec used to visit Ancourt, the printer with whom he worked, at daybreak, so early that the presses were not yet in operation. A virtually sleepless night, spent doing the rounds of the bars, from the smartest to the most sordid, left him with snatches of bawdy songs and a book full of sketches. He slept little or not at all, snatching perhaps a few minutes' rest on the way to the printer, and would then repair to the bar on the corner, where, for all his love of good wine, he was quite capable of ordering the worst rum.

As soon as the cocktail hour arrived, Lautrec, always accompanied by his silent cousin, headed for the Café Weber, his headquarters in the rue Royale, where he was said to consume more spirits in a single evening than the whole of Europe in one day. This was the gathering place of all the capital's writers, musicians, artists, journalists, international celebrities, and popular figures of the moment. Among them was Polaire, a fashionable actress and singer, who drew crowds to the Scala, a well-known café-concert, to see her review *Paris fin de sexe*, featuring a battalion of pretty women, dressed and undressed in rotation. « We were interested by this living Egyptian statuette whose waist could be enclosed in a mere bracelet, » said the poet Paul Leclerq, who was as bowled over as Lautrec by

her astonishing wasplike dimensions. Leclerq wrote a song for her which became famous in America; Lautrec immortalized her in a lithograph. They used to meet around the little mahogany tables at Weber's.

Other regulars included Charles Maurras, Léon Daudet, and Forain, whose thunderous laugh drowned the conversation, also Georges Feydeau and Willy, Colette's first husband. Lautrec and Curnonsky, the well-known writer on gastronomic subjects, exchanged ideas on food, while Claude Debussy smoked long cigarettes from the East. Oscar Wilde, his felt hat pulled low over his eyes, occasionally disappeared into the back room, which was known as « L'Omnibus. » He had suffered deeply from the case brought against him because of his relationship with a young English lord. Sometimes, the collar of his coat half turned up, his pockets stuffed with magazines and books, ever looking for someone he never found, Marcel Proust would make his appearance amid the clouds of cigarette smoke, then retrace his steps, push through the door, and vanish. This list of the famous would be incomplete without mention of the prince of aesthetes and greatest dandy of all, Robert de Montesquiou. Like Lautrec, he was a native of southwest France, through his ancestor d'Artagnan.

Lautrec attributed the most extraordinary and unsuitable occupations to passing customers, judging by their appearance. If he did not like the look of them, and they happened to be sitting near him on the moleskin seats, he would give them a look of exasperation and move away, muttering enigmatically into his beard : « Raclette... ». Only his close friends had any clue to the meaning of his epithets, curt phrases, and sarcastic sallies, which he would intersperse with Languedoc dialect and a highly individual play on words.

When it came to choosing drinks, Lautrec's fastidiousness came to prominence. At Weber's it did not occur to him to drink anything other than vermouth and port, playing poker dice for the saucers. Although the game was forbidden in the café, Charles, the friendly head waiter, turned a blind eye as he smilingly did the rounds, attending to his customers. By the sixth or seventh glass there was always someone ready to declare that it was time to eat. « The last glass » was

*Previous double page :
elegant society went to the
Opéra on Mondays, to the
Français on Tuesdays.
Lautrec, a regular member
of the audience, delighted
in seeing the fops and
soubrettes in repertory at
the Français. He attended
the Variétés thirty evenings
in a row to see a comic
opera, every line and tune
of which he knew by heart,
breaking open bottles of
champagne from his
observation post in a box.*

*THE CHAP BOOK, 1895. An
advertisement designed for
an English publisher.
England exported to Paris
drivers, jockeys, bookmakers,
cocktails, ham, and roast
beef. The sign of a grand
lifestyle was to have one's
laundry done in London.
The Café Anglais was a
smart social meeting place.
But it was in the Irish and
American Bar that Lautrec
met revelers like himself
and the Rothschilds'
driver Tom.*

then drunk, and golden pâtés en croûte and sandwiches were brought to the table, accompanied by pints of pale ale or stout. Often Lautrec would choose instead to eat Welsh rarebit.

In the same street, at the same time, members of the racing world, jockeys included, flocked to the Irish and American Bar. This was where Lautrec came when the Weber was overcrowded or he found his fellow customers excessively pretentious. The horsey atmosphere reminded him of everything he liked about England. The bar was wellknown in racing circles, among the men in tweed jackets described by Debussy as « people in checks. » In the long, narrow, smoky room, a single row of tables faced the mahogany bar, propped up by morose drunkards lost in contemplation of jars of pickles and posters of the Grand Prix. « It's as beautiful as a Rembrandt, » exclaimed « Monsieur le comte marquis, » as Achille, the owner, used to address him with lighthearted grandiloquence. Ralph, who officiated behind the bar, was a true professional. Of Chinese and American Indian descent, a native of San Francisco, he was expert at the preparation of night cups, rainbow cups, mint juleps, and cherry cobblers, all as pleasing to the taste as to the eye. Transfixed on his seat, Lautrec adventurously tried them from seven o'clock at night to ten o'clock in the morning, sometimes later, while admiring the supple movements of the barman's wrists, tapering fingers, and unfailingly accurate movements. Despite the general clamor of the room, the simple utterance of the name « Ralph » in a voice the barman knew well was enough to bring him with a refill.

While the Rothschilds dined at Maxim's or the Café de Paris in the avenue de l'Opéra, the most fashionable restaurants, their coachman Tom was a pillar of the nearby Irish and American Bar, where he drank at the counter. The clowns Footit and Chocolat came there after performing at the Nouveau Cirque, where one of them danced to the music of the other's banjo. In the bar's very « London » atmosphere, Lautrec was to be found in the company of May Belfort, with whom he was romantically involved. This Irish singer, always accompanied by a black cat, had been discovered at the Décadents. She owed her success as much to her

CHOCOLAT DANSANT DANS LE BAR D'ACHILLE (CHOCOLAT DANCING IN ACHILLE'S BAR), 1896. _Footit and Chocolat were a famous pair of clowns, as inseparable at the bar as in the ring of the Nouveau Cirque. Their buffoonery greatly amused customers of the Irish and American Bar, who here include Whistler, recognizable by his strand of hair and cane. Lautrec often came to dine at the bar after the show with Jane Avril, May Belfort, and a few friends. The Welsh rarebit was the best in Paris._

133

LA LOGE AU MASCARON
DORÉ (THE BOX AT THE
THEATER WITH THE GILDED
MASK), *1893. An assiduous
theatergoer, Lautrec
brilliantly captured the
atmosphere of the
auditorium, its elegance, its
opulence, its magic aura.
To illustrate the program
for Marcel Luguet's*
Missionaire, *performed at
the Théâtre Libre in 1893,
he portrayed the English
artist Charles Edward
Conder sitting next to an
elegant redhead dressed in
black, who viewed the play
through a pair of opera
glasses.*

*Right : there is no
mistaking the air of a
Parisienne — the way she
winds her boa around her,
enters the theater door,
descends the red-and-gold
corridors, and unbuttons
her gloves before heading
for her box, where she will
be better seen; the way
she lingers over the
program and looks
seductively around at her
neighbors...*

touching fragility as to her repertoire of folk ballads. Lautrec was captivated by the unhealthy air and fatal charm of this lanky, seemingly languorous girl, who reminded him of an orchid. Joyant compared her much less poetically to a toad.

Wherever he went, Lautrec exercised his powers of observation. Whether at a cycling track, theater, circus, or dance, he noticed every gesture, movement, and attitude of those around him, and transcribed them on paper, filling his pockets with sketches for future paintings.

He knew all the smells of the cafés at different times of day, the aromas of frying eggs and steaming onion soup, the pungency of beer, the whiff of aniseed in absinthe.

Lautrec could not resist cabarets. A favorite was the Chat Noir, a little room furnished with an assortment of objects, where singers sang ribald songs to bourgeois customers out for a taste of the low life, where the barmen gave themselves scholarly airs, and the drinks were memorable. « I have had a most amusing time these last few days at the Chat Noir. We arranged for an orchestra, and made everyone dance. It was very entertaining, but we didn't get to bed till five in the morning, » he wrote to his mother in 1886.

He frequented theaters, more because of their atmosphere than their performances. In a confidential vein, he said to the art critic Arsène Alexandre : « The theater's good even when it's bad, it still amuses me. » He was capable of spending twenty evenings in a row in the same place, simply to admire the sculptural back of the actress Marcelle Lender, who starred triumphantly in *Chilpéric*. In the same spirit, entranced by its Japanese elements, he attended performances of *Papa Chrysanthème*, a spectacular ballet that was much talked about. Under moving spotlights, dancers in diaphanous costumes undulated around a lake covered in lotus flowers.

Lautrec drank constantly. As Thadée Natanson remarked, « He does not give his mustache time to dry. » His alcoholic tendencies gave him a taste for food that stimulated the thirst, such as herrings in onion, little cheese toasts, rum tarts. To escape the surveillance of Paul Viaud, who had been appointed by his

family to keep an eye on him, Lautrec secretly ordered a hollow cane in which he kept a supply of alcohol — a ruse that was very quickly discovered.

Fortunately he recovered with astonishing ease, no doubt helped by his ability to doze off under any circumstances. When he went to London in 1898, for an exhibition of his work opened by the Prince of Wales, he fell asleep on a gallery bench. Confronted by the somnolent artist, the prince asked that he should not be woken up. After visiting Lautrec in his studio, Arsène Alexandre, his faithful critic, observed : « Such is the intense vitality of this supposedly doomed man, such the reserves of strength in this so-called freak, that the very people who believed he was headed for destruction have been left stupefied by his remarkable recovery. »

Those close to Lautrec nonetheless saw undeniable signs of ill health, which obliged him to undergo treatment. In 1899, after an attack of delirium tremens, he was interned in Doctor Sémelaigne's clinic where he spent eleven weeks. There he was condemned to the intolerable dreariness of « harmless and very refreshing » soda water.

Before quitting this life, and the world of good food that had played so important a part of it, Lautrec could not resist indulging an extreme streak of black humor. This took the macabre form of a recipe for grilling a saint to test his saintliness. « Try to procure a real saint through the agency of the Vatican. Treat him as Saint Lawrence was treated on August 10, 258. Having whipped him, put him on the grill over a large bed of charcoal. Like his predecessor, if he is a real saint, he will himself ask to be turned over to be perfectly grilled on both sides. »

At the end of his physical resources, utterly cast down, all Lautrec wanted was to go home to his mother at the Château de Malromé. His last picture, of his « minder » Paul Viaud, was left unfinished. A few days before his death, which took place on September 9, 1901, a letter from his father in Paris to René Princeteau described Henri's condition with great emotion. « I plan to leave tonight at the earliest or tomorrow at the latest to see my poor son Henri, who is drained of all strength and can no longer eat anything at all :

he quietly drinks a little port and some rum grogs. What strength can one hope he will gain from these drinks, which have already poisoned him, such quantities has he drunk in the past ? For some months his legs have been unable to carry him : he dragged himself about, but his arms held out and he managed to paint with zeal ; yesterday he asked for his easel and brushes again, but his hands would not answer his bidding. »

Right : well-known caterers, such as Potel and Chabot, delivered all sorts of cold food during the inverval : plates of petits fours, dishes of canapés, chicken in aspic, elaborate desserts, and other assorted delicacies.

136

Lithograph for Reine de Joie *by Victor Joze, 1892.*

Recipe Book

André Daguin
with the assistance of Yves Pinard

All the recipes serve
4-5 people unless
otherwise indicated.

saffron, and a dash of vinegar or lemon juice. This sauce with its interchangeable ingredients is usually served with fish; but if your fish happens to be pickled, it is best to omit the vinegar/lemon juice.

SAUCE JAUNE DITE
« MAÎTRE D'HÔTEL »
(« _Maître d'Hôtel_ » _Yellow Sauce_)

9 oz (250 gms) butter
Juice of 1 lemon
Parsley
Salt and pepper

Over a low flame heat 9 oz of butter with the chopped parsley, salt, pepper, and juice of one lemon.

SAUCE AU VIN JAUNE ORANGE
OR SABAIONNE/
ZABAGLIONE/SABAYON
(_Sabayon Wine Sauce_)

6 eggs
½ cup (10 cl) white wine or sherry or port
6 tsps (120 gms) sugar

Beat well six egg yolks. Stir in two small glasses of good white wine, port, or sherry and 6 tsps. of sugar. Stir this continuously over a very low heat until the sauce thickens.

SAUCE JAUNE ORANGE FONCÉ CURRY
(_Dark Orange Curry Sauce_)

1 oz (30 gms) fresh Bayonne ham
2 eggs
5 oz (120 gms) butter
½ oz (15 gms) flour
4 ½ cups (85 cl) stock
1 onion

1 bunch parsley
1 tbsp curry powder

Take half the butter, a finely chopped onion, a bunch of parsley, and the chopped ham; gently sauté together until the onions are soft. Stir in the flour, curry powder, and stock. Stir well, boil for 15 minutes, and strain.

Boil the strained sauce for a few minutes; then remove from the heat and stir in two egg yolks that have been blended with the remainder of the butter.

SAUCE RÉMOULADE VERTE ET JAUNE
(_Green and Yellow Remoulade Sauce_)

2 ½ cups (50 cl) mayonnaise
¾ oz (20 gms) capers
1 oz (30 gms) pickles
Parsley, chervil, and tarragon

Add chopped parsley, chervil, tarragon, capers, and pickles to a mayonnaise sauce.

SAUCE VERTE
(_Green Sauce_)

2 ½ cups (50 cl) mayonnaise
1 oz (30 gms) each watercress, parsley, chervil, tarragon, and chives

Pound together the chervil, tarragon, parsley, chives and watercress leaves. Stir this into a mayonnaise sauce.

SAUCE VERTE ET BLANCHE
AUX CÂPRES
(_Green and White Caper Sauce_)

2 oz (50 gms) butter
2 oz (50 gms) flour
2 ½ cups (50 cl) fish stock

3 oz (80 gms) capers
Juice of 1 lemon

Stir together the flour and butter in a saucepan over a gentle heat. Moisten with fish stock or plain water, and stir until nearly boiling. Immediately remove from the heat and add salt, pepper, capers, and the juice of one lemon.

SAUCE ROUGE DITE « PAUVRE HOMME »
(Red Sauce, or « Poor Man's Sauce »)

3 tsps red wine vinegar
1 shallot
¼ medium-sized onion
Parsley

Stir together in a small bowl three teaspoons of good red wine vinegar, some finely chopped parsley, onion, or shallot, and freshly ground pepper. Serve with oysters or shellfish.

SAUCE ROSE-ROUGE
(Pink Sauce)

2 oz (50 gms) butter
2 oz (60 gms) flour
2 ½ cups (50 cl) stock

To a sauce of blended butter, flour, and stock, add cooked tomato purée; puréed sea-urchin coral; puréed crab coral; melted butter that has been colored with the cooking water from shrimp, she-crabs, crayfish, lobster; or pounded anchovies.

WELSH RAREBIT CLASSIQUE
(Classic Welsh Rarebit)

For twelve rarebits :
3 slices bread

5 oz (125 gms) of Cheshire cheese
½ oz (15 gms) butter and oil for frying
½ glass beer
½ oz (15 gms) English mustard
Salt and pepper

Cut each slice of bread into quarters and fry in butter.
Mix the butter and grated cheese in a saucepan and stir over a low heat until the cheese has completely melted. Add the beer, a little at a time, followed by the mustard. Boil for 2 minutes, remove from the heat and season with salt and pepper. Pour over the fried toast and serve.

RINGTUM TIDDY

For sixteen small toasts :
4 slices sandwich loaf
2 cups tomato purée
1 tsp (5 gms) salt
2 tsps (10 gms) sugar
1 pinch pepper
1 finely chopped onion
2 oz (50 gms) grated Gruyère cheese
1 oz (25 gms) butter

If you are serving Ringtum Tiddy as a first course, use a square, pre-cut sandwich loaf.
Mix all the ingredients together and add a pinch of salt, pepper, and a little English mustard.
Cut thin bread slices into quarters and butter well. Then spread with the mixture and place in a buttered oven dish. Cook under a grill or in a hot oven for 5 minutes and serve sprinkled with a little paprika.

CROÛTES AU FROMAGE
(Cheese on Toast)

Slices of «ficelle» bread
(baguette in its thinnest form)
7 oz (200 gms) Gruyère cheese
1 tbsp (10 gms) goose fat

Cut the ficelle into thin rounds; then cut the Gruyère into thin slices of the same size and shape.

Grease a heavy-bottomed skillet with goose fat and lay the pieces of bread in it. Brown on both sides. Lay the cheese on the bread rounds and cover the frying pan. Cook very slowly. The bottom of the bread should be toasted, and the cheese melted, in about 4-6 minutes. Serve immediately.

BEDFORD TOAST

3 slices sandwich bread
2 large slices cooked ham
Breadcrumbs
1 ¹/₂ oz (45 gms) Gruyère cheese
1 oz (25 gms) butter

Slice the bread thinly and lay the ham on top. Sprinkle with grated Gruyère mixed with breadcrumbs. Add a generous knob of butter and grill in a hot oven.

Bedford toast is known as « croque-monsieur » in France.

CANAPÉS D'HUÎTRES « À CHEVAL »
(Angels on Horseback)

For twelve bite-sized pieces :
3 slices sandwich bread
12 oysters
2 large slices cooked ham
2 oz (60 gms) butter
Salt, white pepper, and cayenne pepper

Toast the bread, cut into quarters, and cover each canapé with a piece of ham that has been cut to fit it exactly. Place an oyster on each piece, sprinkle with cayenne pepper and freshly ground white pepper, and top with a pat of butter. Cook for about 3 minutes in a hot oven or under a salamander.

PÂTÉS DE FROMAGE
(Cheese Pâtés)

1 lb 10 oz (800 gms) stale bread
4 oz (100 gms) butter
10 oz (300 gms) grated Gruyère cheese
2 cups (40 cl) consommé
16 eggs
¹/₂ cup Armagnac
Salt and white pepper

In a gratin dish, place the slices of stale bread, buttered and covered with grated cheese, to three quarters of the height of the dish. Cover with a mixture made from the egg yolks, consommé, and Armagnac in the proportion four yolks to half a cup of consommé and one-eighth cup of Armagnac. Add a little salt and white pepper. Top with a generous layer of grated Gruyère. Cook for 45 minutes in the oven in a bain-marie.

Leave to cool and serve in slices. Serve cold, or heat up under a salamander or in a hot oven.

SALADE DE TRUFFES ET MÂCHES AU SAUTERNES
(Truffle and Mâche Salad with Sauternes)

For 2 people :
3 truffles of ¹/₂ oz (10-15 gms) each
2 eggs
1 glass Sauternes
1 tsp peanut oil
1 small tender carrot
4 oz (100 gms) mâche (lamb's lettuce)
Salt and white pepper

Wash the mâche and dry. Carefully brush the truffles and cut them into fine slices.

Make a vinaigrette using the Sauternes instead of vinegar. Mix with it a chopped hard-boiled egg yolk.

Serve the vinaigrette onto the individual plates, and then place the mâche followed by the truffle rounds on top. Sprinkle with the egg yolk and chopped carrot. Two turns of the pepper mill (white pepper), and the salad is ready : simple and delicious.

Truffle and mâche salad with Sauternes.

GOUGÈRES BOURGUIGNONNES
(Bourguignon Cheese Pastries)

2 oz (50 gms) butter
Salt
5 oz (150 gms) flour
3 whole eggs
3 oz (80 gms) Gruyère cheese

Into a heavy-bottomed saucepan pour two large glasses of water, two tablespoons softened butter, and two pinches of salt. Bring to a boil and add the sifted flour all at once. Beat continuously over the heat (as for puff pastry) until the mixture follows the stirring spoon.

Remove from the heat and add three whole eggs and the diced Gruyère, stirring vigorously all the while.

On a well-buttered oven sheet, at 2-in. intervals, lay a tablespoon of this mixture — as round as possible (exactly as for cream puffs). Cook for 25 minutes at 425° F.

TARTE AUX POIREAUX ET À LA MOELLE
(Leek and Marrow Pie)

12 oz (350 gms) salted shortcrust pastry
2 ¼ lbs (1 kg) leeks
9 oz (250 gms) beef or veal marrow
5 cups (1 l) stock
2 oz (50 gms) butter
1 ¼ cups (25 cl) cream
1 ¼ cups (25 cl) milk
4 whole eggs
Grated nutmeg
Salt and pepper

Roll out the pastry into a circle $\frac{1}{8}$-in. thick. Press the pastry lightly into a pie pan. Place a sheet of buttered aluminum foil over the pastry and weigh down with dried beans. Cook for 10 minutes in a hot oven.

Remove the green part of the leeks, slice the white parts, and wash thoroughly. Heat the butter and sweat the leeks for 10-15 minutes, but do not allow to color. Season with salt and pepper.

Poach the marrow 3-5 minutes in the simmering stock; then drain on absorbent paper.

Mix together the cream, milk, and eggs and season with nutmeg, salt, and pepper.

Place the leeks in the pre-cooked pie crust, add half of cream mixture and cook for 5 minutes. Add the remaining mixture and cook for another 25 minutes in a hot oven.

During this time, cut the marrow into rounds. Arrange these on top of the pie for the last 2 minutes in the oven.

FOIE GRAS

1 duck foie gras of 1-1 $\frac{1}{2}$ lbs (500-600 gms)
5 cups (1 l) milk
$\frac{1}{2}$ cup (10 cl) Armagnac
3 $\frac{3}{4}$ qts (3 l) duck stock

Take the foie gras and remove any greenish part that may have come in contact with the bile; also remove the membrane of the skin and the blood vessels. To do this, slice the liver cleanly lengthwise.

Now place the liver in salted milk, to which the Armagnac has been added, and leave for 36 hours in the refrigerator. Drain, wash, and mold the liver into a sausage shape in wax paper. Wrap this tightly in a clean tea towel and tie up each end with string.

Cook for 20 minutes in barely simmering clarified duck stock; chicken stock will do.

Cool immediately in iced water after wringing out the tea towel twice.

DAUBES DE CÈPES AU VIN BLANC
(Bolete Mushrooms Stewed in White Wine)

12 oz (350 gms) lean Bayonne ham
12 medium-sized bolete mushrooms
4 oz (100 gms) goose fat
1 garlic clove
Parsley
$\frac{1}{4}$ cup (15 cl) Piquepoult white wine
$\frac{1}{2}$ cup (10 cl) water

Choose a dozen firm, medium-sized boletes and brush them clean (do not wash). Remove the stems and peel them. Sauté the mushroom caps in the hot goose fat for about 30 minutes in a heavy-bottomed skillet. Salt and pepper sparingly as boletes do not take well to pepper.

Meanwhile chop the ham finely with the bolete stems, garlic, and parsley. Remove the bolete caps from the skillet, replace with the chopped mixture, and fry in the same goose fat. Moisten with the dry white wine. When the wine begins to boil, add a little hot water (though not as much as the wine).

Place the mushroom caps delicately on top of this mixture and cook gently until they begin to subside. Adjust seasoning and serve on a well-heated platter.

OMELETTE AU ROQUEFORT
(Roquefort Cheese Omelet)

1 oz (30 gms) butter
2 oz (50 gms) cream
2 $\frac{1}{2}$ oz (70 gms) Roquefort cheese
9 eggs

Blend together the cream and the cheese, and leave to stand in a warm place — where the mixture should soften but not liquefy entirely.

Beat the eggs and pour them into the hot melted butter in the skillet. As the omelet begins to cook, add the cheese-cream mixture, stirring gently so that it blends well with the eggs.

When the omelet is done, slide it gently from the skillet into a serving dish, at the same time folding it over into a proper omelet shape.

MULLIGATAWNY SOUP

10 oz (300 gms) diced cooked chicken
4 oz (100 gms) butter
2 ½ qts (2 l) chicken stock
5 oz (150 gms) flour
12 onions
Curry powder and saffron

Melt the butter and gently brown a dozen chopped onions for about 20-25 minutes. Sprinkle with the flour, a tablespoon of curry powder, and a pinch of saffron stamens.

Stir continuously for at least 10 minutes until the flour is cooked. Stir in the chicken stock and let it simmer for a good hour.

Skim and degrease the soup and pour it into soup plates over the diced cooked chicken.

SOUPE À L'OIGNON ET À l'AIL OU « LA CUISINE AVEC PRÉMÉDITATION » *(Garlic and Onion Soup, or Premeditated Cooking)*

4 oz (100 gms) butter
4 oz (100 gms) duck fat
5 oz (150 gms) flour
12 onions
12 garlic cloves

In a large, heavy-bottomed copper cooking pot, melt the butter and add to it half the flour, stirring

all the while. When it is thoroughly mixed, add the chopped garlic and onions.

Continue stirring with a wooden spoon while adding the remaining flour. Cook this very gently for a good hour, stirring whenever necessary to avoid sticking or burning, until the mixture has formed a thick paste. Place this paste in an earthenware bowl that you have first rinsed with boiling water. Seal the top with the duck fat.

This miraculous potion can transform plain water into a delicious broth if added in the proportion of 2 tbsps to the quart.

What is more, it is delicious with toast — the original fast food!

SOUPE DE MARRONS *(Chestnut Soup)*

3 dozen chestnuts, shucked and peeled
2 clean leeks (white part only)
1 peeled onion
1 heaped tbsp (20 gms) butter
5 cups (1 l) chicken stock
1 bouquet garni
1 cup (20 cl) crème fraîche
4 slices toast
Salt and pepper

Chop the leeks and onion and sauté gently in butter for 10 minutes, but do not allow to color. Add the chestnuts, the bouquet garni, and the stock. Season with salt and pepper and cook for about 45 minutes.

Remove the bouquet garni and put the mixture through a blender. Return to the cooking pot, gradually add the cream, and let it cook gently for a further 10-15 minutes. Serve topped with toast that has been fried in goose fat.

SOUPE À L'AIL
(Garlic Soup)

12 garlic cloves
2 slices bread
Thyme and cloves
5 oz (150 gms) goose fat
Peppercorns
2 eggs

Peel the garlic, sticking one of the pieces of garlic with three cloves, and place in a cooking pot with three sprigs of thyme, a little salt, and twelve peppercorns. Add five cups (1 liter) of water and boil rapidly for half an hour.

Strain the soup through a chinois, pressing down firmly to extract the garlic juice. Bring the soup back to the boil and whip in two whole eggs.

Serve in soup plates over toasted bread fried in goose fat.

SOUPE AUX ABATTIS D'OIE
(Goose Giblet Soup)

2 ¹/₂ qts (2 l) beef stock
Goose giblets (head, neck, wings,
feet, gizzard, heart, etc.)
Nutmeg
2 oz (50 gms) pearl barley
Salt and pepper

Soak the barley in warm water for 30 minutes or so.

Place the giblets with the barley in the beef stock (from a stew for example) and simmer for 1 hour.

Strain the soup and pick the meat off the bones. Adjust the seasoning, grate a little nutmeg, add the pieces of goose, reheat, and serve.

SOUPE AUX FÈVES
(Broad Bean Soup)

2 ¹/₄ lbs (1 kg) broad beans
6 onions
2 carrots
12 celery stalks
1 handful green beans
1 handful green peas
Savory
1 oz (25 gms) flour
2 oz (40 gms) duck fat
Salt and pepper

Shuck the fresh broad beans, which should be young and tender enough not to need peeling. Empty them into the boiling water. Add salt and pepper, four white onions, the chopped celery, a carrot cut into rounds, the peas, and the green beans, along with a sprig of savory, and a handful of peeled broad beans — these will thicken the soup. Cook for 1 hour on a low heat.

In a heavy-bottomed saucepan, sauté in duck fat, two chopped white onions, and a carrot cut into rounds. Sprinkle with the flour and stir well. Add 4 ¹/₂ cups (1 liter) of the cooking liquid from the beans. Bring to the boil, add to the soup, and cook steadily for another hour.

POTAGE ALBIGEOIS DE PRINTEMPS
(Albigeois Spring Soup)

4 oz (100 gms) lard
3 turnips
3 leeks
3 tomatoes
1 onion
1 celeriac
7 oz (200 gms) Bayonne ham
Goose fat
Croûtons
Salt and pepper

Place the roughly chopped ham in a heavy-bottomed cooking pot with the lard and the goose fat. Add the chopped vegetables and brown them. Add 3 quarts (2 ½ liters) of water, cover, and cook gently for a good hour. Season with salt and pepper.

Serve with croûtons fried in duck fat.

CONSOMMÉ À LA QUEUE DE BOEUF
(Oxtail broth)

1 oxtail
About 1 lb (450 gms) carrots
9 oz (250 gms) onions
9 oz (250 gms) leeks
9 oz (250 gms) turnips
7 oz (200 gms) celery stalks
12 garlic cloves
1 beef marrowbone
3 cloves
Bouquet garni
Salt and peppercorns

Slice the oxtail into sections and tie the pieces together.

Cut one onion in half and grill it to color the consommé. Put the grilled onion, the rest of the onions stuck with cloves, carrots, leeks, turnips, celery, garlic, and marrowbone in a stock pot. Cover with 6 quarts (5 liters) of cold water. Add salt in moderation, add six or seven peppercorns and the bouquet garni. Bring to the boil, skim off the impurities that rise to the surface, and leave to simmer for 3 hours.

After 30 minutes take out the marrowbone, remove the marrow, reserve it, and return the bone to the stock.

Strain the stock through a fine cloth, add a glass of old port, and serve very hot over slices of beef marrow.

DORADE À LA GELÉE
AU COURT-BOUILLON LIÉ
(Jellied Sea Bream)

1 sea bream of 2 ¼ lbs (1 kg), or 2 of 1 lb each
7 oz (175 gms) flour

½ cup (10 cl) olive oil
3 qts (2 ½ l) water
5 oz (150 gms) carrots
2 onions
1 or 2 shallots
1 garlic clove
1 celery or fennel stalk
Quatre épices
Salt and pepper

Clean, scale, and slice the sea bream into sections. Season with salt, pepper, and quatre épices, and leave to stand for 2 hours.

Make a roux with the flour and olive oil; add the water, pepper, chopped carrot, onions, shallots, garlic, celery or fennel, and cook for a good hour. Leave aside to cool.

Place the sea bream in a cooking dish and cover with the thickened stock; simmer for about 30 minutes.

Move the fish to a deep platter; reduce the stock and pour it over. As it cools, it will form a jelly.

This dish is served cool but not ice-cold and can be accompanied by a hot vegetable. Toulouse-Lautrec would probably have eaten it with fried potatoes.

BROCHET AU VIN ROUGE EN GELÉE
(Jellied Pike Cooked in Red Wine)

3 ¼ lbs (1.5 kg) pike with the head cut off
(or a pike of over 4 ½ lbs, 2 kg intact)
12 lardons (bacon chunks)
12 garlic cloves
3 onions
2 carrots
1 turnip
1 calf's foot
2 tbsps tomato concentrate
3 tomatoes
1 head celery
Sprig of tarragon
1 bottle red Bordeaux wine
Salt and white pepper

Clean and scrape the pike and dot it with the bacon and nine blanched garlic cloves. Season with salt and pepper.

Prepare a braising base by sautéing the chopped vegetables and the three remaining garlic cloves with the 2 tbsps of tomato concentrate. Lay this mixture on the bottom of a large, heavy oven dish; place the pike on top.

Cook, along with the head which will supply the gelatin, for about 2 hours in a medium oven (375°F). After the first 10 minutes, add the wine, which has first been warmed.

Baste at least three or four times in the course of the cooking. After 2 hours, move the fish to a large serving platter. Strain the cooking liquid through a chinois, pressing the head well to extract as much gelatin as possible. Reduce this liquid for 10 minutes and pour over the fish.

Allow to cool, then place in the refrigerator for 2 to 3 hours before the « sacrifice. »

SAUTÉ DE LOTTE À LA CRÈME D'AIL DOUX ET DE CITRON
(Monkfish with Creamed Garlic and Lemon Sauce)

1 lb 10 oz (800 gms) monkfish fillets
12 garlic cloves
3 lemons
2 1/2 cups (50 cl) single cream
3/4 oz (20 gms) truffles
1 cup (20 cl) fish stock
2 1/2 cups (50 cl) duck fat
4 oz (100 gms) flour
2 tbsps chopped chives
2 or 3 shallots
1/4 cup (5 cl) white wine
2 oz (50 gms) butter

Wash the lemons thoroughly and peel. Separate the yellow part (zest) from the white part (zist). Finely slice the zest and blanch for 2 minutes in boiling water. Drain and set aside.

Peel the garlic and cook it in the duck fat along with the zist. When the garlic is well done, drain and add it to the cream along with the zist. Boil for 2 minutes, purée in a food processor and set aside.

Cut the fillet of monkfish into 1/2-in. thick medallions, roll them in flour and fry them in a nonstick pan until they are very lightly browned. Remove them from the pan and reserve. Sweat the chopped shallots in butter and deglaze with the white wine. Reduce to practically nothing; then add a quarter of the garlic-lemon sauce. Bring to the boil, add the fish, and heat for 1 or 2 minutes.

Place in the middle of a serving dish, nap with the remaining sauce, sprinkle with a julienne of lemon peel, truffles, and chopped chives.

RAGOÛT DE LOTTE ET HOMARD TOUT SIMPLE
(Simple Stew of Lobster and Monkfish)

1 lb 10 oz (800 gms) fillet of monkfish
cut in medallions
1 lobster of about 1 lb (450 gms)
(preferably from Brittany)
1/4 cup (5 cl) single cream
5 oz (150 gms) chopped chives
5 oz (150 gms) butter
1/2 cup (10 cl) Noilly Prat
1/4 cup (5 cl) olive oil
2 carrots
1 onion, 1 shallot
1 leek

Cut the monkfish into medallions and keep cool.

Put together a court-bouillon for the lobster; when it starts to boil, put in the lobster and cook for 8-10 minutes. Remove, drain, pick out the flesh reserving the claws, and set aside.

In another saucepan put the olive oil, Noilly Prat, a little of the lobster stock, the chopped shallot, salt, and white pepper. Bring to the boil and add the medallions of monkfish. After 3 minutes add the lobster claws and the meat from the lobster tail cut in medallions. Cook for another minute.

Arrange the slices of monkfish in a flower pattern on a serving plate. Place the medallions and lobster claws on top and keep hot.

Add the cream to the juice, bring to the boil, and reduce rapidly. Add the butter, stirring continuously, season, and pour over the lobster and fish. Sprinkle with chives and serve piping hot with a good fruity white wine.

COQUILLES SAINT-JACQUES À L'AIL CONFIT
(Scallops with Stewed Garlic)

8 scallops
20 garlic cloves
¹/₂ cup (10 cl) goose fat
¹/₃ cup (8 cl) olive oil
3 oz (80 gms) butter
Salt and pepper

Select good-sized scallops. Open them and clean them well, taking care to remove all trace of the « beard. »

Stew the garlic in the simmering goose fat until done. Strain.

Sauté the scallops in the hot olive oil, season with salt and pepper, and cook for about 5 minutes on a high temperature.

Place two scallops in each shell along with four garlic cloves. Pound the remaining garlic into a purée and add it to lightly browned butter. Nap the dressed scallops with this garlic-butter sauce.

HARENGS POUR BIEN BOIRE
(Herrings to Raise a Thirst)

6 smoked herrings
¹/₂ cup (10 cl) milk
¹/₂ cup (10 cl) peanut oil
3 oz (80 gms) strong mustard
7 oz (200 gms) breadcrumbs
8 turnips
¹/₂ cup (10 cl) vinegar
Half a lemon
Salt and pepper

Scallops with stewed garlic.

Peel the herrings (not an easy task!) and leave them in a bowl under a slowly running tap overnight.

Fillet them, dry them on absorbent paper, then oil them, rub them with mustard, and roll them in the breadcrumbs.

Peel and grate the turnips into a pulp, cover them with milk, and leave them to marinade for 15 minutes. Drain this pulp and season it with salt, pepper, and lemon juice.

Arrange the turnip pulp at the bottom of an oven dish and cook for 10 minutes at 400°F. Remove from the oven and set aside where it will stay warm.

Grill the fillets in the oven for 10 minutes. Arrange the herrings on top of the turnip purée, grind some fresh pepper on top, and serve.

MORUE AUX POIREAUX
(Cod with Leeks)

3 ¼ lbs (1.5 kg) salt cod
About 1 lb 2 oz (500 gms) leeks
(white part only)
3 onions
1 garlic clove
5 oz (150 gms) goose fat
1 oz (30 gms) flour
Salt and pepper

Trim the piece of cod with scissors and desalt as usual by leaving to soak in fresh water for 24 hours. Blanch the leeks for 10 minutes and fry in goose fat with the cod, which has been cut up into 1-in. cubes. Set aside and keep warm.

Sauté the chopped onions in goose fat and gradually add the flour, stirring well until it begins to color (about 5 minutes). Add the chopped garlic and a little water. Stir well, add the leeks, and cook gently for 30 minutes.

Just before serving, add the pieces of cod, mix well, and serve piping hot.

ALOSE À L'OSEILLE
(Shad with Sorrel)

1 shad of about 2 ¼ lbs (1 kg),
scaled and cleaned
2 ½ qts (2 l) white wine
Thyme, bay leaf, parsley
2 shallots
Juice of 1 lemon
3 handfuls sorrel
2 oz (50 gms) butter
½ cup (10 cl) crème fraîche
2 oz (50 gms) flour
⅓ cup (7 cl) cooking oil
Salt and pepper

Crosshatch the skin of the shad with a sharp knife, and leave for an hour in a marinade of dry white wine, lemon juice, salt, pepper, chopped shallot, chopped parsley, thyme, and bayleaf.

Clean the sorrel and chop coarsely. Sweat the sorrel in a saucepan with a knob of butter and a little water until it is reduced to a purée. Stir in the flour, salt, and pepper. When this is all well incorporated, add a ladle of crème fraîche and cook gently for 30 minutes.

Remove the shad from the marinade and dry it well. Oil the fish and then grill it on a very hot grill that has been well scrubbed beforehand. Turn it over after 6 minutes; then bake in a hot oven for a further 8 minutes.

Cover the bottom of a serving dish with the sorrel purée, lay the fish on top, and serve.

FILETS DE SOLE À L'ESTRAGON
(Fillets of Sole with Tarragon)

2 soles of about 1 ½ lbs (600-700 gms) each
3 shallots
½ cup (10 cl) white wine
½ cup (10 cl) crème fraîche
5 oz (150 gms) butter
4 oz (100 gms) tarragon
4 oz (100 gms) carrots
4 oz (100 gms) shallots
Salt and pepper

Peel and fillet the soles. Sweat the bones with the minced shallots and carrots. Moisten with white wine and 1 ¼ cups (¼ liter) of water, and cook for 20 minutes.

Strain through a chinois and reduce by three quarters. Chop the tarragon leaves, mash them into the butter, add the cream season with salt and pepper, and place in a bain-marie.

Fold the fillets of sole over four times, making small incisions on the edges with a kitchen knife where necessary, in order to bend the fillets. Place them in a buttered baking dish, season with salt and pepper, add the wine, and cook for 10 minutes in a hot oven. Arrange the fillets on a serving dish and nap with the sauce.

ALOSE SANS ARÊTE
(Boneless Shad)

1 shad of 3-3 ¼ lbs (1.2-1.5 kg)
5 cups (1 l) vinegar
1 calf's foot
5 oz (140 gms) Bayonne ham
Lemon
5 cups (1 l) white wine
1 glass gin

Clean, scale, and trim the fish, and leave it to soak for 10 minutes in the vinegar. Bone the fish; with a pair of tweezers remove as many small bones as possible (i.e. the ones that spread out on either side of the backbone).

Cut the fish into three or four pieces and leave in vinegar for 2-3 hours; the bones that you have not been able to remove with tweezers should be softened or dissolved by the vinegar.

Lay barding fat or bacon in the bottom of a thick-bottomed cooking pot, along with the calf's foot and a handful of diced ham; place the pieces of fish on top. Cover the fish with slices of lemon from which the pips have been removed, and pour over the wine and gin.

Cover, sealing the top, and place in a slow oven for the afternoon.

This is delicious — in theory, all the fish bones should dissolve because of the acidity of the sauce.

MATELOTE D'ANGUILLE
(Eel Stew with White Wine)

1 large eel (2 ¼-2 ½ lbs/1 kg-1.2 kg)
1 bottle dry white wine
1 glass eau-de-vie
1 tbsp (5 cl) crème fraîche
2 eggs
3 garlic cloves
Thyme and bay leaf
2 shallots
24 baby white onions

Knob of butter
Salt and pepper

Have the fishmonger skin the eel. Chop it into sections and place these in a dish with salt, pepper, and eau-de-vie. Set aside for 5 to 6 hours.

Melt the butter in a saucepan and gently sauté the baby onions. When they begin to brown slightly, add ¼ cup of water and cook for 10-15 minutes. Set aside and keep warm.

Crush the garlic and cook in the wine, together with the sliced shallot, thyme, and bayleaf. Season to taste, boil for 30 minutes, and strain the hot juices over the chunks of eel in a casserole. Bring back to the boil and simmer for 15 minutes, then remove the eel and keep warm.

Add the crème fraîche to the remaining liquid and reduce for 4-5 minutes. Stir in the butter and the egg yolks vigorously; remove from heat and continue stirring. Pour over the eel, arrange the baby onions around the dish, and season with freshly ground pepper before serving.

COQUILLES SAINT-JACQUES
À L'AIL CONFIT
(Scallops with Garlic)
(Variant)

Flesh and coral of 36 large scallops
12 garlic cloves
2 oz (50 gms) butter
Salt and pepper
1 tbsp duck fat

Peel the garlic cloves and cook them slowly (30 minutes) in duck fat, then drain them, while still hot, through a strainer.

Heat 1 tbsp of duck fat and a knob of butter in a casserole, then add the flesh of the scallops and brown each piece for 4-5 minutes on either side.

Season with a pinch of salt and plenty of white pepper, then add the garlic and the coral. Swirl very briefly over the heat and serve immediately.

BROCHETTES D'HUÎTRES AU FOIE GRAS
(Brochettes of Oysters and Foie Gras)

24 oysters
14 oz (400 gms) fresh duck foie gras
½ cup (10 cl) of Noilly Prat
2 ½ cups (50 cl) crème fraîche
¾ lbs (300 gms) carrots
1 lb 2 oz (500 gms) leeks (white part only)
Chopped chervil
Salt and pepper

Make a julienne with the carrots and the white part of the leeks. Chop the shallots. Open the oysters and remove them from their shells, saving the liquid from the oysters. Cut the foie gras into about twenty-four cubes of around ¾ in. (2 cms).

Assemble the brochettes, alternating oysters and foie gras (six oysters and six pieces of foie gras per person is about right). Pepper the brochettes freely ; then reduce the Noilly Prat, the shallots, and the liquid from the oysters, and squeeze firmly through a cheesecloth.

Poach the julienne in the reduced sauce, and add the cream. Cook the julienne in the cream ; then reduce the cream to the smooth consistency of a velouté.

Season the sauce if necessary, then place the brochettes in it to cook : 2 minutes should suffice.

Lay the julienne in the bottom of a dish, with the brochettes on top ; pour the remaining sauce over them and sprinkle with chervil before serving.

BARBUE AU VIN ROUGE ET GROSEILLES
(Brill with Red Wine and Redcurrants)

3 lbs (1.5 kg) brill
1 bottle red wine
9 oz (250 gms) onions
7 oz (200 gms) carrots
7 oz (200 gms) leeks
1 ½ cups (25 cl) demi-glace
2 ½ oz (100 gms) butter

8 oz (225 gms) redcurrants
Bay leaf, parsley, thyme
Salt and pepper

Fillet the brill and remove the skin. Stew the bones in a mirepoix of onions, carrots, and leeks, then add the wine and the bouquet garni and allow to simmer for 15 minutes. Filter the liquid through a chinois and reduce by about one quarter. Add the demi-glace (i.e. the greatly reduced bouillon). Reduce again, this time by half.

Salt and pepper the fillets of fish and steam them for 10 minutes. In the meantime, complete the sauce by bringing it back to the boil and adding the butter, whipping it to a foam as you do so. Finally, add the redcurrants to the sauce, boil for a few seconds, and serve hot over the fish.

HOMARD FLAMBÉ
(Flambéed Lobster)

For two people :
1 lobster of about 2 ¼ lbs (1 kg)
3 ½ oz (100 gms) butter
½ cup (10 cl) olive oil
½ cup (10 cl) Armagnac
7 oz (200 gms) carrots
7 oz (200 gms) onions
¾ lb (400 gms) tomatoes
2 ½ cups (50 cl) white wine
2 ½ cups (50 cl) crème fraîche
Bouquet garni
Flat-leaved parsley
Salt and cayenne pepper

Plunge the lobster in boiling water to kill it, then split the head longways and cut each section in two. Then slice the tail into medallions and crack the armor of the legs and claws with pliers. Reserve the juice.

Sauté in very hot butter and olive oil ; then flambé generously with Armagnac, afterwards adding a mirepoix of carrots, onions, and crushed tomatoes. Next add the white wine and the bouquet garni, salt and pepper. Simmer for 5 minutes.

Remove the pieces of lobster, place them in a serving dish, and keep warm.

Reduce the sauce considerably and add the lobster juice. Then strain through a chinois over the lobster, sprinkle with parsley, and serve.

BARBUE CANCALAISE
(Brill Cancale-Style)

1 brill of 4.4 lbs (2 kg), cleaned and prepared
2 dozen flat oysters
¹⁄₂ cup (10 cl) cream
8 oz (225 gms) flour
1 ¹⁄₄ cups (25 cl) white wine
1 lemon
Bouquet garni
1 onion
1 carrot
1 leek
Garlic
Knob of butter
Salt and pepper

Open the oysters; filter and set aside their juice. Make a sauce base (fumet) with the fish head and trimmings in a saucepan, using the white wine and an equal quantity of water. Add the white part of a leek, a carrot cut into quarters, the bouquet garni, a clove of garlic, an onion, salt, pepper, and the juice of one lemon. Bring to the boil and simmer for 45 minutes. Allow to cool and strain through a chinois.

Pour the cold fumet over the fish and bring very slowly to simmering point; cover and place in a very slow oven or over an extremely low flame, and leave to cook for about 15 minutes. Remove the fish, scrape off the black skin, and place on a serving dish, taking care to clean all round it. Set aside and keep warm.

Make a béchamel sauce using the fish fumet and the liquid from the oysters; thicken this with the cream. Add the oysters and poach for a few seconds; remove them and place around the fish. Pour over the sauce and serve immediately.

ÉCREVISSES À LA GUYENNAISE
(Guyenne-Style Crayfish)

36 crayfish
¹⁄₂ cup (10 cl) duck or goose fat
3 onions
3 carrots
Knob of butter
7 oz (200 gms) Bayonne ham
2 glasses Armagnac
5 cups (1 l) dry white wine
Sprig of tarragon
Salt and cayenne pepper

Crayfish are considered ready to eat when their feet are red — and good to eat when they are heavy.

Clean them by twisting the middle of the end of the tail, and pulling; this should bring out the entire black intestine in one piece.

When you have done this, place the crayfish in a thick-bottomed copper pan and heat them until their color turns to red. Then flambé them generously with the Armagnac. Add the duck or goose fat, the carrots chopped together with the ham and onions, and a sprig of fresh tarragon. Cook over a medium heat for 10 minutes or so, before adding the white wine. Bring to the boil, allow to cook quickly for a further 6 minutes, then remove the crayfish and set aside: they are now cooked.

Continue simmering the sauce for a further half hour; it will thicken unaided, because of the vegetable fibres it contains. Season with Armagnac, cayenne pepper, and salt to taste. Remove the tarragon, pour the sauce over the crayfish, heat briefly, and serve.

Note : Absinthe, if you have it, can be used as a substitute for both the Armagnac and the tarragon.

BROCHET FARCI
(Stuffed Pike)

1 large pike of 3-3 ¼ lbs (1.2-1.5 kg)
2 slices stale bread
4 oz (100 gms) mushrooms
3 anchovy fillets
1 egg
Green olives
Salt and pepper

Clean and prepare the fish, setting aside the head; season with salt and pepper and place in the refrigerator.

In a food processor, blend together the slices of stale bread dipped in left-over gravy from a roast, a handful of fresh mushrooms, the anchovies, egg, and as many olives as you like. Season to taste and fill the cavity of the pike with this mixture. Wrap tightly in aluminum foil that has been greased on the side touching the pike and bake in a medium oven (325-375°F) for at least 1 hour. The result will be just as good if you double the cooking time, since the foil will keep the fish moist.

HUÎTRES ALCOOLISÉES AU GENIÈVRE
(Oysters in Gin)

20 oysters
2 oz (50 gms) shallots
1 oz (25 gms) chives
½ cup (10 cl) gin

Open the oysters, pour off their juice, and place them in the refrigerator for half an hour.

Chop the shallots and chives, and macerate for half an hour in the gin.

Serve the oysters on a bed of crushed ice with a teaspoon of sauce on each one.

MORUE AUX HARICOTS BLANCS
(Salt Cod with White Beans)

¾ lb (450 gms) salt cod
7 oz (200 gms) dried white beans
2 onions
2 garlic cloves
3 oz (80 gms) goose fat
Salt and pepper

Desalt the cod by placing it in fresh water for 24 hours; then poach gently without boiling. Drain, skin, and shred the pieces with your fingers.

Boil the beans (after soaking them overnight in fresh water). Do not add salt; this tends to harden their skins.

Sauté the chopped onions and garlic in the goose fat, using a thick-bottomed pan. When golden, add a little of the bean water and a few spoonfuls of crushed beans, and stir together. Add the remaining beans and the cod, mix well, and allow to cook for 15 minutes over a moderate heat. Check the seasoning before serving.

GIGOT TREMPÉ
(Marinaded Leg of Lamb)

For 8 people :
1 large leg of lamb (about 7 lbs or 3.5 kg)
6 garlic cloves
1 bottle red Gaillac wine
4 shallots
Bay leaf and thyme
Juniper berries
Knob of butter
1 oz (25 gms) flour
4 oz (100 gms) goose fat
Salt and pepper

Stud the meat with slivers of garlic.

Boil the red wine for 45 minutes with a tablespoon of salt, a teaspoon of pepper, a dozen juniper berries, bay leaf, thyme, and the peeled shallots sliced lengthways. When this marinade has cooled, pour it over the leg of lamb and allow to stand for 36-48 hours, turning the meat from time to time so the marinade can penetrate evenly.

Remove the lamb, wipe dry, and place in a roasting pan. Grease it well with goose fat, sprinkle with salt and pepper and cook in a very hot oven for 70 minutes, plus 10-15 minutes in the same oven after the heat has been turned off.

While the lamb is cooking, prepare the sauce. First, melt the butter in a pan; as soon as it froths, scatter the flour over it and cook until the mixture reddens slightly; then slowly incorporate the strained marinade. Bring to the boil, then simmer for 30 minutes and check the seasoning. Place the lamb in a serving platter and serve the sauce separately in a gravy boat.

PETIT RAGOÛT DE PINTADE AUX GIROLLES
(Guinea Fowl Stewed with Girolles)

1 guinea fowl
³/₄ lb (450 gms) of fresh girolle mushrooms
2 shallots
¹/₂ cup (10 cl) Madeira
³/₄ cup (15 cl) demi-glace
1 ¹/₂ cups (30 cl) crème fraîche
Knob of butter
Knob of duck fat
1 ¹/₂ oz (30 gms) chopped chives
1 sprig of dill
Salt and pepper

Draw the guinea fowl and debone the breast parts. Cut each of the drumsticks and thighs into two pieces and each of the wings, with the breast attached, into three.

Dress the pieces well with salt and pepper, and place in a preheated skillet with duck fat, adding the girolles (wiped clean, *not* washed in water, and with only the very largest cut in two). When both mushrooms and meat are well-browned, pour off any excess fat.

Soften the shallots in the pan, deglaze with Madeira, then add the demi-glace and the cream. Cover and allow to cook very slowly for 15-20 minutes only. When done, put aside the pieces of guinea fowl and the mushrooms, keeping them hot.

Reduce the sauce a little, add butter, salt, and pepper, and set aside, keeping hot.

Arrange the ragoût in the center of a platter with the girolles distributed around and on top of it. Nap with sauce, adding chopped chives and a sprig of dill at the last minute.

PIGEON RÔTI AUX BULBES EN CHEMISE ET GIROLLES
(Roast Pigeon with Girolles and Shallots in their Skins)

For two people :
1 pigeon
6 shallots in their skins
6 garlic cloves
2 oz (50 gms) chopped parsley
2 oz (50 gms) foie gras
5 oz (20 gms) sliced shallots
7 oz (200 gms) girolle mushrooms
2 oz (50 gms) duck fat
2 oz (50 gms) chopped shallots
¹/₄ cup (5 cl) white wine
¹/₄ cup (5 cl) demi-glace
2 oz (50 gms) butter
¹/₄ cup (5 cl) cream
Salt and pepper

Prepare the pigeon for cooking. Make a stuffing of the chopped pigeon's liver, parsley, the sliced shallots, and the foie gras; fill the cavity of the pigeon with this mixture, season with salt and pepper, and truss with string.

Next, sear the pigeon quickly on all sides in a little fat, then cook in the oven for 10-15 minutes depending on its size, adding the garlic cloves and shallots in their skins.

When the pigeon is cooked (the flesh should be slightly pink), remove from the pan and keep hot in a covered casserole, together with the shallots and the garlic.

Pour off the fat, add the chopped shallots, and cook until slightly golden. Deglaze with the white wine ; then reduce the liquid and add the demi-glace. Reduce very slightly and add cream. Reduce yet again and remove from the heat. Check seasoning and put the sauce aside in a saucepan.

Prepare the girolles by cutting off their stems — *do not wash them* in water.

Heat some duck fat in a skillet and add the girolles (only the largest ones should be cut in two). Cook briskly for 2-3 minutes, then put aside.

Finally, take an oval copper pan and place the pigeon in the middle of it, arranging the garlic, shallots, and girolles around it. Sprinkle the whole with 2-3 spoonfuls of the thickened sauce and serve, accompanied by the remaining sauce in a gravy boat.

ROSACE DE MAGRET
AUX ÉCHALOTES CONFITES
(Duck Breast with Shallots)

2 duck magrets
20 small shallots
2 ¹/₂ cups (50 cl) duck fat
2 oz (50 gms) chopped shallots
¹/₂ cup (10 cl) red wine
¹/₄ cup (5 cl) demi-glace
¹/₄ cup (5 cl) cream
2 oz (50 gms) butter
14 oz (400 gms) green cabbage
4 oz (100 gms) diced smoked bacon
3 garlic cloves
¹/₂ cup (10 cl) duck fat
Salt and pepper

Skin the shallots and cook very slowly in the 2 ¹/₂ cups of duck fat for about an hour.

Clean the cabbage, discarding the tough outer leaves, slice as thinly as possible and put aside.

Heat some more fat in a sauté pan, then add the bacon and brown over a low heat; add the sliced cabbage and the crushed garlic cloves. When done, drain in a colander and keep hot.

Prepare the magrets, sprinkle with salt and pepper, and fry in a skillet for 8-10 minutes, skin side down. Turn over and cook for 4 more minutes (they should be pink inside). Pour off excess fat, add the whole shallots, and cook gently until soft. Add the red wine and reduce; add the demi-glace and reduce again for 2 minutes. Add the cream; remove from the heat as soon as it begins to bubble; stir in the butter, salt and pepper, and set aside, taking care to keep the sauce warm.

Lay the cabbage in a platter with the sliced magret arranged on top in a flower pattern; garnish with shallots and sauce.

AILLADE DE VEAU À LA GASCONNE
(Veal and Garlic à la Gasconne)

2 ¹/₄ lbs (1 kg) shoulder of veal
2 oz (50 gms) lard
5 garlic cloves, peeled and chopped
1 onion, peeled and minced
1 bouquet garni
3 tomatoes dipped in boiling water,
peeled, and seeded
2 cups stock
3 oz (80 gms) breadcrumbs
1 tsp sugar
Salt and pepper

Dice the veal into cubes of about an inch. Place the tomatoes in the oven to dry for 5 minutes.

Brown the veal with the lard in a heavy-bottomed cooking pot. Add the chopped garlic and cook for 5 minutes before adding the chopped onion, the bouquet garni, salt, and pepper.

Remove the tomatoes from the oven and add to the meat, along with the hot stock. Bring to the boil, check seasoning, add a teaspoonful of sugar, cover, and leave to stew very gently for 3 hours.

Place in an ovenproof platter, sprinkle with breadcrumbs, heat in the oven for 5 minutes and serve.

LA POULE VERTE
(Green Chicken)

9 oz (250 gms) cured ham
9 oz (250 gms) lard or bacon
12 oz (350 gms) pork
12 oz (350 gms) veal
9 oz (250 gms) crustless bread
3 eggs
5 cups (1 l) milk
1 large frisé cabbage
7 oz (200 gms) lard
3 ¼ lbs (1.5 kg) potatoes
Salt and pepper

Chop very finely by hand (or in a food processor) the ham, bacon, pork, and veal. Blend in the bread previously soaked in milk. Season with salt and pepper.

Blanch the cabbage for 6 minutes in boiling salted water. Remove the outer green leaves and set them aside for later use. Chop the heart of the cabbage and add to the stuffing mixture with three eggs that have been beaten with a little milk.

Sprinkle the stuffing well with pepper and mold into an oval shape.

Spread a clean dishcloth on the table and lay on it the large outer leaves of the cabbage, each overlapping the next by half. Roll up the stuffing in the cabbage leaves and tie up in the dishcloth. This is your « green chicken. »

Fill with water a cooking pot large enough to contain the « chicken, » the potatoes, and the lard ; bring these ingredients to the boil and simmer for 90 minutes. Adjust seasoning.

After 90 minutes, untie the « green chicken » on a serving platter and surround with the potatoes ; the privilege of carving it should go to the guest of honor.

POT-AU-FEU CONSOMMÉ FROID
(Pot-au-feu served cold)

1 shin of veal
1 shin of beef

1 chicken of about 3 ¼ lbs (1.5 kg)
4 garlic cloves
2 eggs
6 carrots
6 onions
9 oz (250 gms) cured ham, half-fat, half-lean
2 shallots
Crustless bread
1 green cabbage
6 turnips
6 leeks
2 glasses Madeira

Stuff the chicken with a well-seasoned mixture of finely chopped (by hand) ham, garlic, shallots, the chicken's liver, and heart bound with two beaten eggs, and three slices of stale, crustless bread that has been soaked for 2 hours in milk.

Dip the beef and veal shins in boiling water and then rub them well with salt and garlic. Place them, along with the chicken, in a deep, thick-bottomed stock pot which will contain 10-12 qts of water in addition to the other ingredients. Add the vegetables, which should all be good-sized.

Cook the pot-au-feu, or casserole, very slowly, skimming the froth off the surface frequently to start with. After 2 hours, add the Madeira and test the meat for tenderness with a needle : if the needle penetrates without difficulty, it is done. Remove each piece of meat as soon as you judge that it is ready, and place in a large, heavy tureen, which has been preheated. Strain the stock through a sieve and then through a fine cloth. Reboil it very quickly to cook the smaller vegetables that you have set aside for eating at the table. Pour the vegetables and stock over the meat and serve. (Leftover stock can be put aside for later use as cold consommé.)

PÂTÉ DE LAPIN ARTIFICIEL
(Imitation Rabbit Pâté)

For 12 people :
1 lb 10 oz (800 gms) veal

14 oz (400 gms) fresh lean bacon
14 oz (400 gms) lean pork
14 oz (400 gms) sausage meat
7 oz (200 gms) Bayonne ham
1 broad strip barding fat (or sliced bacon)
5 cups (1 l) white wine
4 medium-sized truffles
1 onion
2 shallots
8 cloves
Thyme and bay leaf
1 bouquet garni
Pinch of nutmeg
Salt, pepper, and a few whole peppercorns

Marinade four long, lean, flat scallops of veal (each one large enough to cover the bottom of your earthenware terrine) in a mixture of good white Bordeaux wine, salt, pepper, spices, nutmeg, bouquet garni, minced onions, shallots, and carrots.

In the bottom of a terrine 10 in. in length, put a few cloves, three bay leaves, some sprigs of thyme, nutmeg, and peppercorns. On this bed of herbs and spices spread enough sliced bacon or barding fat to fold back over when the terrine is filled, taking care to cover the sides very well. Now add the following ingredients, layer by layer : the veal, cut lengthways into five or six narrow strips ; between each strip a band of Bayonne ham, a band of unsalted lean bacon, and a band of lean pork. Season with salt and pepper, and cover with a layer of sausage meat mixed with a very little finely chopped onion and shallot and fragments of truffle. Repeat the process for the next layer, distributing the truffles in large pieces around the meat, until the terrine is filled completely. Fold over the barding fat (or bacon) and compress the meat, slipping cloves and bay leaves between the sides of the terrine and its contents. Lay sliced onion, shallots, bay leaf, a sprig of thyme, and some peppercorns on top, cover with foil or greaseproof paper, and close the terrine tightly, using a paste of water and flour to seal the lid.

Bake in a very slow oven for at least 3 hours, then allow to cool for a further 3 hours. Finally, turn out onto a dish (you will find this easier if you warm the sides of the terrine) and serve.

ENTRÉE DE VEAU A LA GASCONNE
(Veal à la Gasconne)

4 ½ lbs (2 kg) topside of veal
7 oz (200 gms) Bayonne ham
12 white onions
2 carrots
2 oz (50 gms) flour
Duck fat
½ cup (10 cl) tomato sauce
2 ½ cups (50 cl) meat stock
Nutmeg, ginger, clove
1 stick celery
Salt and pepper

Brown the veal in the duck fat and place it in a casserole large enough to contain it with the lid on.

In the pan used to brown the veal, sauté the onions and the carrots chopped into rounds, sprinkling them with a little flour as you do so. Allow the flour to cook for 5-6 minutes to make it digestible, then add the tomato sauce. Simmer for 5 minutes, then pour over the veal.

Deglaze the pan with 2 ½ cups of meat stock and pour it boiling hot over the veal. Season lightly with salt, add pepper and a little fresh ginger sliced en julienne, a clove, and the celery stalk. Cover and cook slowly for 2 hours, then dip the ham quickly in boiling water, cut it into cubes, add to the veal, and cook for 2 more hours. Correct seasoning, sprinkle with half a ground nutmeg, and serve.

OIE BRAISÉE À LA STRASBOURGEOISE
(Braised Goose à la Strasbourgeoise)

1 fat goose
10 oz (300 gms) lean pork
7 oz (200 gms) country bread
1 ½ cups (25 cl) milk
Parsley and marjoram
10 carrots
10 onions
2 ½ cups (50 cl) white wine
2 ½ cups (50 cl) chicken stock

3 oz (80 gms) butter
Salt and pepper

Soak the bread in milk for 2 hours and mash with a fork. Add to it the minced pork, the chopped parsley, salt, pepper, and marjoram. Mix the ingredients but not overmuch.

Stuff the goose with this mixture, sew the cavity shut, and brown on all sides.

In a roasting pan large enough to contain the goose, spread a layer of carrots and onions cut into rounds, and place the bird on top. Sprinkle with water and place in a hot oven.

After 25-30 minutes, pour in the white wine, cover with foil, and roast for at least one more hour (or more, depending on the size of the goose).

When thoroughly cooked, remove the goose from the oven, carve, and put aside to keep warm. Add the chicken stock to the juice in the pan and reduce for 10-15 minutes. Adjust seasoning, strain through a chinois into a gravy boat, and serve as an accompaniment to the goose.

PERDREAUX COMME EN PÉRIGORD
(Partridges Périgord-Style)

4 partridges
1 onion
3 shallots
2 ¼ lbs (1 kg) bolete mushrooms
4 chicken livers
1 cup (20 cl) stock
3 oz (75 gms) lean Bayonne ham
1 egg
Crustless bread
4 oz (100 gms) duck fat
5 oz (125 gms) bacon
Chopped parsley
Salt, pepper, and spices

Set aside the caps of the boletes; wipe the stems clean, chop with the onion and shallots, then toss briefly in very hot duck fat to seal in the flavor.

Beat the egg and mix with the chopped chicken livers and ham, adding the chopped parsley and a little bread dipped in stock. Season generously (with plenty of pepper).

Mix the two stuffings together and cram each partridge tightly with the mixture. Truss well, taking care to sew the cavities shut.

Dice the bacon, blanch, and sauté with the partridges in duck fat until brown. Fry the sliced and seasoned bolete caps in very hot fat (it should be smoking), then turn them into the pan containing the partridges. Cover with foil and cook for 30 minutes in a slow oven (320°F).

Add a tablespoon of stock, sprinkle with parsley, heat quickly on the stove, and bring to the table immediately.

OIE FARCIE
(Stuffed Goose)

1 goose
1 lb 2 oz (500 gms) sausage meat
7 oz (200 gms) barding fat or bacon
Half a calf's foot
10 onions
10 carrots
2 shallots
Garlic
3 ¾ cups (75 cl) stock
A bottle and a half dry white wine
Salt and pepper

Cook gently in butter a chopped onion, one crushed clove of garlic, and two chopped shallots. When soft, drain, turn into a casserole with half a bottle of wine, and reduce by two-thirds.

Poach the goose's liver (which is *not* a foie gras), pound it in a mortar, and mix it with sausage meat. Add the marinade and some chopped parsley. Stuff the goose with this mixture after seasoning well with salt and pepper.

Close the cavity and sew shut; truss the bird and place it in an earthenware stewpot, on a bed of roughly chopped barding fat or bacon with finely chopped carrots and onions cut into rounds. Set around the goose the roughly chopped calf's foot. Add the bottle of dry white wine and a little stock, and leave to cook gently for 3 hours in the oven, basting from time to time.

When the goose is done, remove to a platter and extract string. Degrease the stock, strain through a chinois, and reduce over a high heat, serving in a gravy boat as an accompaniment to the goose.

If you serve this dish with braised or boiled cabbage, do not degrease the stock — it will improve the taste of the cabbage immeasurably.

SAUTÉ DE VEAU MARENGO
(Veal Marengo)

3 ¼ lbs (1.5 kg) round roast of veal
3 oz (75 gms) lard
3 onions
5 oz (150 gms) flour
2 garlic cloves
1 cup (20 cl) white wine
12 small onions
6 tomatoes
Parsley
Salt and pepper

Cut the veal into cubes of about 1 in. and cook lightly in lard. When about half-cooked, pour off most of the fat, add the chopped onions, and allow to soften for a few minutes before stirring in the flour. Cook the flour well to make it more digestible; then season and add the peeled, seeded, and crushed tomatoes, the white wine, and (as soon as this mixture comes to the boil) a glass of water. Add the bouquet garni and the garlic, cover and leave to cook in a medium oven. After an hour, remove the cover and cook for a further 15-20 minutes.

Brown the small onions gently in butter; then arrange the cooked (i.e. tender) meat in a deep dish. Jettison the bouquet garni, add the onions, reduce the sauce until fairly thick, then turn the meat back into it and gently reheat to near boiling point. Correct seasoning, transfer back to the platter, sprinkle with parsley, and serve directly.

GIGOT D'AGNEAU DE SEPT HEURES
(Seven-Hour Leg of Lamb)

3 ¼ lb (1.5 kg) leg of lamb
2 ¼ lbs (1 kg) cucumber
2 ¼ lbs (1 kg) zucchini
1 lb (450 gms) tomatoes
1 lb (450 gms) onions
2 dozen garlic cloves
5 qts (4 l) beef stock
3 oz (75 gms) butter
Thyme flowers
Salt and pepper

Debone the leg of lamb, leaving only the shinbone, and stud well with garlic cloves.

Using a high-sided cooking pot, or (even better) a braising pan, brown the lamb on all sides in butter. Add the diced vegetables and the thyme flowers.

Season with salt and pepper, half-fill with boiling beef stock, cover, and cook in the oven at 300°F for 7 hours.

Check every 30 minutes that there is sufficient liquid, and stir the vegetables well to ensure even cooking, adding more stock whenever necessary.

Serve the lamb directly, using a spoon to scoop off the meat. Serve the juice and vegetables directly from the pot.

GRAS-DOUBLE DU BUGEY
(Tripe with «Marc de Bugey»)

2 ¼ lbs (1 kg) blanched tripe
1 deboned calf's foot
5 tomatoes
4 sliced onions
Bouquet garni
½ cup (10 cl) marc de Bugey (or other marc)
4 oz (100 gms) lard
Knob of butter
2 bottles white Chardonnay
Salt and pepper

Slice the tripe and sauté the pieces in a pan with the calf's foot, in very hot lard, until well-browned. Drain and move to a casserole.

Flambé with a little marc de Bugey — the warmer it is, the better it will flare.

Cook the sliced onions in butter and add them to the tripe, along with the tomatoes cut into quarters and the bouquet garni. Simmer very gently for at least 1 $\frac{1}{4}$ hours then add white wine and continue to cook gently for a further 2-3 hours.

Remove the bouquet garni and serve in the same casserole.

CRÉPINETTES
(Little Flat Sausages encased in Caul)

12 pigs' feet
9 oz (250 gms) fat pork sausage meat
7 oz (200 gms) pig's caul
2 carrots
2 turnips
2 $\frac{1}{4}$ lbs (1 kg) onions
18 carrot sticks
18 celery sticks
18 French beans
1 $\frac{1}{2}$ cups (25 cl) cream
1 garlic clove
2 cloves
1 tbsp good mustard
1 bottle white wine
Peppercorns

Blanch the pigs' feet for 5 minutes in boiling water, then scrub them off under the cold tap. Cook gently in a well-seasoned court-bouillon for 2 hours. Leave to cool in the court-bouillon, then remove all bones and place in the refrigerator overnight.

Blanch the sticks of carrot and celery for a few minutes, along with the beans. Arrange over the pigs' feet and cover with a thin layer of fatty sausage meat to hold them in place.

Next envelop the feet in the caul, spread with mustard, and sprinkle with breadcrumbs. Fry on both sides in pork fat and transfer to a platter in a warm oven. Pour away the cooking fat, deglaze with three tablespoons of vinegar, add fresh cream, mustard, and crushed peppercorns.

Serve with an onion purée.

NAVARIN DE MOUTON
(Navarin of Mutton)

4 $\frac{1}{2}$ lbs (2 kg) mutton
4 oz (100 gms) lard
3 onions
2 oz (50 gms) flour
Bouquet garni
1 tbsp tomato concentrate
2 garlic cloves
2 $\frac{1}{4}$ lbs (1 kg) small round turnips
Salt and pepper

Cut the meat (shoulder, neck, or belly) into large pieces and fry in lard in a thick-bottomed casserole. Remove from the heat when well-browned and keep warm.

Jettison the fat (beware, real mutton yields plenty of it). Add the sliced onions, cook for a minute or so, then stir in the flour and allow to cook for 5 minutes more. Add the garlic, the bouquet garni, and a spoonful of tomato concentrate, and put the meat back in the pan. Add water to cover, season with salt and pepper, bring to the boil and cook in a medium oven for 30 minutes with the lid on.

Remove the bouquet garni and add the peeled turnips. Cook for another 35 minutes.

Correct the seasoning, take out the pieces of meat and put them in a deep serving dish. Reheat the sauce, remove more fat if necessary, pour over the meat and serve.

« FALETTE, »
OU POITRINE DE VEAU FARCIE
(*« Falette, » or Stuffed Breast of Veal*)

1 breast of veal
4 oz (100 gms) fat bacon
7 oz (200 gms) veal scallop
7 oz (200 gms) Swiss chard (green part only)
4 oz (100 gms) breadcrumbs
4 onions
Quatre épices
2 eggs
1 pork rind
1 small green cabbage
3 carrots
3 ¼ lbs (1.5 kg) pink-skinned potatoes
4 oz (100 gms) lard
1 cup (20 cl) white wine
2 ½ cups (50 cl) veal stock
6 garlic cloves
Salt and pepper

Make a farci (forcemeat) by chopping together the fat bacon and the veal scallop. Add to it the sliced green Swiss chard, chopped onions, the dried breadcrumbs, salt, pepper, and a pinch of quatre épices. Bind with two beaten eggs.

Open the veal breast and fill the middle of it with the stuffing; then roll it up and tie it well.

In a thick stewpot, place the pork rind and the veal breast, with the cabbage cut into quarters, the carrots and two onions cut into rounds. Pour white wine over these ingredients, bring to a boil, lower the heat, and add the boiling stock. Cover and cook for 3 hours in the oven.

Cut the breast into round slices and arrange on a hot serving dish. Strain the cooking juices, pressing hard to extract as much liquid as possible. Degrease, adjust the seasoning, pour over the veal, and serve with potatoes and garlic sautéed in lard.

DUO DE MAGRETS EN COQUE DE SEL
(*Magrets of Duck in a Salt Crust*)

2 duck magrets
4 ¼ lbs (2 kg) kosher salt
4 oz (100 gms) flour
10 egg whites
4 oz (100 gms) thyme

Trim the magrets, crosshatching the skin with a sharp knife.

Prepare a salt paste with a mixture of flour, salt, thyme, and egg whites.

Heat a skillet and sear the magrets on their skin sides. In the meantime, place a layer of kosher salt half an inch thick on the bottom of an oiled oven dish. When the skin of the magrets is well browned, put them together fleshside to fleshside and envelop them in salt paste. The crust should form an airtight shell, which will harden during the cooking.

Place the « Duo » in a hot oven (390°F) for 20 minutes. It is best to leave the shell unopened for another 10-15 minutes before serving.

POULARDE EN ESTOUFFADE
DU QUERCY
(*Smothered Chicken, Quercy-Style*)

1 chicken, drawn and trussed
2 ½ oz (70 gms) lard
7 oz (200 gms) bolete mushrooms
6 slices Bayonne ham
1 truffle
1 qt (75 cl) chicken stock
Flour
Salt and pepper

Brown the chicken in hot fat, then cook very slowly for 20 minutes.

Wipe the bolete mushrooms with a dry cloth; do *not* wash them. Slice the boletes and the truffle separately.

Place the chicken in an earthenware terrine, the bottom of which is covered with slices of the ham.

In the pan used for browning the chicken, and using the same fat, sauté the boletes for 15 minutes. Then arrange them around the chicken, in a terrine, along with the chopped truffle. Season with salt and pepper, then add the boiling chicken stock. Fold slices of ham over all and cover, sealing the lid of the terrine with a paste of flour and water. Cook in a medium oven (300°F) for 1 hour.

Break the seal and raise the lid (taking care to keep fragments of paste from falling into the terrine), and serve immediately.

BLANQUETTE DE VEAU
(Blanquette of Veal)

24 pieces shoulder of veal (4 ¹/₂ lbs-2 kg)
18 turnips
18 leeks (white part only)
18 small new onions
18 carrots
2 ¹/₂ cups (50 cl) crème fraîche
1 cup (20 cl) white wine

If you own a very thick, very flat-bottomed copper stewpot like the ones at Malromé or the Château du Bosc; if you have both gas and electric cooking facilities; and if you have perfectly mastered the use of all of these things, you may wish to try this recipe for blanquette of veal à sec (dry), which retains all the essence of the meat while yielding a sauce that is no more than the pure, whitened juice of meat and vegetables. The right kind of heavy, enamel-lined pot can sometimes serve just as well as a copper one.

Put all the ingredients in your pot, cover, and cook. Twenty minutes later, remove the turnips, season them with salt, and put them aside in a bowl. Ten minutes later, do the same with the leeks which (if they are really tender) should by now be cooked. Ten minutes later, do the same with the carrots and small onions. The veal will either be ready 20 minutes later or else it will be incinerated (that is, if you have turned the heat even a shade too high).

If all is well, add a little salt and a cup of white wine, reduce to almost nothing, add the cream, and simmer for 10 minutes more (taking out the pieces of meat in the course of this 10 minutes, if they are sufficiently cooked).

TOURTE CHAUDE DE CANARD
(Duck Pie)

1 duck
³/₄ lb (350 gms) pig's jowls
7 oz (200 gms) flaky pastry
1 egg
1 shallot
Nutmeg and hyssop
1 glass Armagnac
1 bottle red Bordeaux wine
Salt and pepper

Debone the duck (preferably a female). Set aside the two breasts, and save the rest of the meat and giblets, including the deboned thighs. Make a stock with the bones : the more meat remaining on the carcass, the better the stock will be. Add the red wine, an equal quantity of water, the Armagnac, and some hyssop, and reduce on a low heat until you are left with less than 2 cups of concentrated stock.

Prepare the forcemeat, using the flesh from the duck's thighs, the pig's jowls, the chopped shallot, a pinch of nutmeg, and a tablespoonful of Armagnac.

Now cut out two rounds of pastry about 10 in. in diameter. Lay the first on an oven sheet, spread half the stuffing over it, then the two duck breasts, and then the other half of the stuffing on top of these. Cover all with the second round of pastry, pinching the edges together; then make a hole in the middle and bake in a moderate oven (325°F) for 30 minutes.

About halfway through the cooking, brush the pastry with egg yolk. Pour the hot concentrated bouillon over the pie just before serving.

TRIPES AU SAFRAN
(Tripe with Saffron)

4 ¹/₂ lbs (2 kg) tripe
1 calf's foot
1 ³/₄ lb (750 gms) carrots
2 ¹/₂ oz (70 gms) garlic
1 bottle white wine
¹/₂ cup (10 cl) Calvados
6 tomatoes
1 egg
4 oz (125 gms) flour
Saffron
Salt and pepper

Cook the tripe and the calf's foot for 7 hours in salted water. Drain and debone the calf's foot.

Select an earthenware terrine that will go into the oven.

Cut the tripe into broad strips, add to it the minced carrots, onions, tomatoes cut into rounds, and garlic. Pour in the white wine and a glass of Calvados. Add salt and plenty of coarse-ground pepper, as well as ten stamens of saffron.

Seal the lid of the terrine with a paste made by mixing 1 egg, 4 oz flour, and ¹/₄ cup of water. Cook in a hot oven for 2 hours.

Serve sprinkled with fresh saffron.

POULARDE EN CHAUD-FROID
(Chaud-Froid of Chicken)

3 ¹/₄ lbs (1.5 kg) chicken
1 truffle (1 oz, 30 gms)
5 oz (150 gms) veal
5 oz (150 gms) sausage meat
1 calf's foot
14 oz (400 gms) onions
7 oz (200 gms) carrots
4 oz (100 gms) leeks
1/2 oz (10 gms) celery
1 heaped tsp chopped chives
3 oz (80 gms) flour
2 oz (50 gms) butter
1 glass port

Take a plump chicken, not too fat, and push slivers of truffle under its skin. Stuff with a forcemeat of half sausage meat, half veal, chopped onions, a little garlic, chives, salt, pepper, and port. Truss tightly.

Poach the chicken with the calf's foot, carrots, onions, leeks, and celery for 50 minutes. Begin this cooking process with the water cold and salted.

After the cooking, allow the chicken to cool in the stock, then drain, setting aside half the stock and reducing the other half.

Make a white roux and stir in the boiling stock strained through a chinois. Adjust seasoning. Leave the chicken in the refrigerator for 1 hour. Let the velouté you have made cool somewhat, then remove the string from the cold chicken, place on a raised grill, and pour the velouté over it.

Transfer to a serving dish with its bottom already swimming in sauce, and decorate as you wish before serving.

HURE D'OIE AUX PISTACHES
(Goose Brawn with Pistachios)

4 preserved goose thighs
9 oz (250 gms) foie gras demi-cuit
2 ¹/₂ cups (50 cl) chicken consommé
1 oz (30 gms) gelatin
1 bunch chopped chives
4 oz (100 gms) shelled pistachio nuts

Boil the consommé, mix in the gelatin, melt, and put aside to cool.

In the meantime, debone the preserved goose thighs and cut into regular-sized pieces. Cut the foie gras into ¹/₂-in. cubes. Scissor the chives and chop the pistachios (not too finely). Mix all these ingredients together and place in an earthenware terrine, taking care not to pack too tightly.

Add the tepid consommé, which will turn to jelly in the terrine. Refrigerate for at least 6 hours. Serve in thick slices with country bread fried and cut into fingers.

MELSAT

4 ½ lbs (2 kg) sausage meat
4 ½ lbs (2 kg) pork belly
15-in. long (40 cm) large sausage casing
(washed pig's intestine)
1 lb 2 oz (500 gms) stale country bread
30 eggs
Salt and pepper

Place in a deep dish five large slices of stale country bread. Add the beaten eggs. Mix together. Allow to rise in a cool place (*not* the refrigerator) for 24 hours.

Add to this mixture the sausage meat and the pork belly, boned and cut into ½-in. pieces. Do this with a knife, by hand, not in the food processor. Season with salt and pepper. Mix well.

Clean the large pork intestines thoroughly and stuff them with this mixture, without filling them entirely. Knot the intestines at both ends; then simmer for 3 hours in salted, peppered water.

Drain and leave to cool between two tea towels.

GRAS-DOUBLE AU SAFRAN À L'ALBIGEOISE
(Tripe with Saffron à l'Albigeoise)

4 ½ lbs (2 kg) beef tripe
¼ cup (5 cl) vinegar
10 oz (300 gms) Bayonne ham
5 oz (120 gms) duck fat
4 oz (100 gms) lard
14 oz (400 gms) carrots
1 head garlic
2 oz (50 gms) flour
5 onions
5 cloves
Bouquet garni
Saffron
Capers and gherkins

Cut up the tripe and put it in a bowl with a glass of vinegar, salt, and one or two onions thickly chopped; knead well with your hands for 10-12 minutes, then wash several times with clean water until the water runs clear.

Place the tripe in a large earthenware (or enameled or cast-iron) cooking pot, along with 6 qts of water, salt, two onions (one spiked with cloves), two or three carrots, a head of garlic and a bouquet garni. Cover the pot and cook in the oven or in front of the fire for at least 5 hours (more if the pot is very thick).

Cut up the ham, both the fat and the lean, into small cubes, and cook in hot duck fat. When the ham has yielded its juice, add one chopped onion; and when this is brown add the flour, stir, allow to cook for a minute or two, then add parsley, chopped garlic, and plain boiling water or water left over from the tripe. Season with salt and pepper, then add the saffron, which you have previously dried and reduced to powder, and the tripe. Cook on a very slow heat for at least 90 minutes. Serve garnished with capers and gherkins.

RÂBLE DE GARENNE DE MONTBAZON
(Saddle of Monbazon Wild Rabbit)

For 2 people :
1 saddle of rabbit
7 oz (200 gms) diced smoked bacon
2 oz (50 gms) melted bacon fat
1 onion spiked with 7 cloves
1 carrot
1 celery stalk
5 garlic cloves
Thyme and bay leaf
⅓ cup vinegar
2 oz (50 gms) flour
24 dried prunes
Beurre manié (1 heaped tbsp butter blended
with 12 tbsp flour)
Fried croûtons
1 bottle red wine

Make a marinade with the onion stuck with cloves, thyme, bay leaf, sliced carrot, celery stalk, 5 cloves of garlic, salt, pepper, vinegar, and a bottle of red wine. Leave the rabbit in this mixture overnight.

Drain the rabbit and brown it in bacon fat, in a cooking pot. Stir in the flour and cook for a further 10 minutes, heating the strained marinade in the interval. Add the marinade to the rabbit and continue to cook gently for 15-20 minutes, depending of the size of the rabbit.

When it is cooked, set aside the meat, keeping it warm. Strain the sauce, then arrange the diced bacon, blanched and sautéed, around the meat.

Remove the stones from the prunes (which have been soaked in wine for 2 hours previously) and add the prunes to the sauce. Reduce the juice in which they have steeped and add to the sauce. Incorporate your beurre manié to the sauce and whip vigorously. Adjust seasoning, and nap the rabbit and diced bacon with sauce. Garnish with fried croutons and serve.

FAISAN À LA CHOUCROUTE
(Pheasant with Sauerkraut)

1 pheasant
1 piece barding fat or bacon
1 glass white wine
2 oz (50 gms) butter
1 petit suisse (cream cheese)
1 lb 10 oz (800 gms) sauerkraut
Bacon and smoked sausage garnish

Pluck, draw, truss, and bard the pheasant, and set it to cook in a closed stewpot with a knob of butter. Remember to put cream cheese in the cavity before cooking. After 20 minutes add a glass of white wine and cook for 20 minutes more.

Serve the pheasant, minus the barding fat, on top of the choucroute, with bacon and sausage as a garnish.

CUISSOT DE CHEVREUIL AUX POIRES
(Haunch of Venison with Pears)

1 haunch of venison (5 lbs, 2.5 kg)
9 oz (250 gms) diced bacon
2 ½ qts (2 l) milk
4 ½ lbs (2 kg) dried pears
Cinnamon
4 oz (120 gms) butter
Salt and pepper

Trim the venison, lard it with the bacon, place in a bowl, cover with milk, and leave to marinate overnight.

Next morning, drain, dry, season, and remove to a roasting pan. Spread all over with butter and place in a very hot oven (470°F) allowing 15 minutes cooking time per pound — and 5 minutes per pound in the warming oven after the cooking is over.

In the meantime, soak the dried pears in a little eau-de-vie de poire (pear) and some ground cinnamon. Just before the cooking is completed, add the pears to the pan along with several knobs of butter. To serve, lay the hot venison in a dish surrounded by the pears, then whip the sauce a little, and pour over.

GRIVES EN COCOTTE
(Thrush en Cocotte)

8 thrush (or quail)
3 oz (75 gms) goose fat
3 juniper berries
1 glass gin
½ bottle dry white wine (preferably Gaillac)
½ cup (10 cl) crème fleurette
1 lb 2 oz (500 gms) fresh pasta

Pluck, draw, and singe the birds, then sear them, in a thick cast-iron pot large enough to contain them all, in smoking-hot goose fat.

Flambé with gin, add two or three juniper berries, cover, and cook until brown (10 minutes). When done, put aside to keep warm, pour the fat out of the pot, and deglaze with white wine (1 glass for 2-3 birds).

Bring to the boil, then add the cream ; bring back to boiling point, then add fresh noodles that have meanwhile been cooked and drained — this requires perfect timing. Couch the birds on the noodles and serve.

CUISSOT DE SANGLIER EN POIVRADE
(Wild Boar's Haunch in a Pepper Marinade)

For fifteen people :
1 haunch of wild boar (8-10 lbs, 4-5 kg)
3 stalks celery
5 carrots
3 onions
2 leeks
3 shallots
1 head garlic
1 bunch parsley
4 bottles red wine
1 ½ cups (30 cl) vinegar
1 ¼ cups (25 cl) oil
5 oz (150 gms) butter
Redcurrant jelly
2 ½ cups (50 cl) thickened veal stock
Thyme, bay leaf, chives
Salt, peppercorns, and ground pepper

Peel the celery, carrots, onions, leeks, and garlic. Wash and chop finely. Place the deboned, trimmed haunch in a large earthenware terrine. Add chopped vegetables, thyme, bay leaf, finely chopped parsley, red wine, salt, cloves, peppercorns, ¾ cup of vinegar, ¾ cup of oil. Marinate for at least two days in a cool place.

Before cooking the meat, drain and place in a roasting pan lined with the vegetables from the marinade, well-drained. Add salt and pepper, and pour the remainder of the oil over the haunch. Cook in a hot oven (390°F) for 2 ¼ hours, turning every 15 minutes.

Meanwhile, take the chopped shallots, the remaining vinegar, 3 tbsps butter, chopped parsley, thyme, bay leaf, salt, and freshly ground pepper, and bring to the boil in a saucepan. Add the thickened veal stock and cook slowly for 45 minutes.

After 2 ¼ hours of cooking, pour 1 ¾ qts (1.5 l) of marinade over the meat and cook for a further 15 minutes. Remove the pan from the oven and set aside the meat, keeping it warm.

Pour the marinade from the roasting pan into a saucepan and add a little redcurrant jelly. Bring to the boil and add the remainder of the butter. Whip vigorously, then strain the gravy through a chinois.

Set the meat on a platter and serve with potatoes sautéed in butter. Serve the gravy separately.

CUISSOT DE CERF
(Haunch of Venison)

Serves eight :
1 haunch of venison (4 ½ lbs-2 kg)
Quatre épices, thyme, bayleaf
1 head garlic (skinned)
6 qts (5 l) beef stock
¼ cup (5 cl) oil
Kosher salt and pepper

Rub the venison well with salt, garlic, quatre épices, thyme, and bay leaf, and leave for 24 hours in the refrigerator, rubbing with the same ingredients from time to time.

Heat the oil in a roasting pan, then brown the meat on both sides. Sprinkle liberally with pepper. Roast in a hot oven (400°F) for 80-90 minutes, basting frequently. Halfway through the cooking, pour off the grease and thereafter baste the meat at intervals with eight cups of stock. In this way the stock will gradually reduce, creating the gravy.

1 lb 10 oz (800 gms) plums
2 ¹/₂ oz (100 gms) sugar

Mix flour, butter, and 1 oz sugar together with a pinch of salt. Add the egg and enough milk to make a soft pastry. Put aside and take an hour's siesta.

Butter a pie dish and line with pastry.

Wash and stone the plums, cut them in two, and lay them skin side down on the pastry, tightly packing them in a circular pattern.

Sprinkle freely with sugar and cook in a hot oven (390°F) for 30 minutes.

TARTE MOELLEUSE AUX FRAMBOISES
(Sticky Raspberry Tart)

12 oz (350 gms) shortcrust pastry
2 whole eggs
2 egg yolks
5 oz (120 gms) sugar
1 cup (20 cl) cream
1 cup (20 cl) milk
1 oz (25 gms) cornflour
1 ¹/₂ cups (30 cl) raspberry juice
¹/₂ cup eau-de-vie de framboise (raspberry)

For the meringue :
2 egg whites
2 ¹/₂ tbsps sugar

Roll out the pastry in a circle, to a thickness of about 1 ¹/₁₀-in. (3mm) ; then line a pie dish with it. Precook pastry for about 10 minutes in a hot oven (390°F).

Place the whole eggs, egg yolks, sugar, cream, milk, cornflour, and raspberry juice in a saucepan and bring to the boil. Remove from the heat and stir in the eau-de-vie de framboise.

Add this topping to the crust and allow to cool a little.

Beat the egg whites and sugar to form a meringue mixture ; spread over the top of the tart and cook for 10 minutes at 390°F.

GRATIN DE FRAISES AU WHISKY
(Strawberry Gratin with Whisky)

1 lb 2 oz (500 gms) strawberries
6 eggs
3 oz (80 gms) sugar
1 oz (20 gms) confectioners sugar
¹/₂ cup (10 cl) whisky
¹/₂ cup (10 cl) crème fleurette

Wash the strawberries, remove their stems, and lay them on a clean cloth to dry. Place them in a deep dish or pie dish.

In a saucepan, blend the egg yolks and the sugar over a very low heat. Add the whisky. When the mixture is frothy and cooked (it should feel thick against the spoon) add the cream, whipped Chantilly-style.

Pour the warm mixture over the strawberries and cook in a preheated oven until lightly browned. Sprinkle with confectioners sugar and serve.

TARTE AU CITRON
(Lemon Tart)

12 oz (350 gms) shortcrust pastry
4 eggs
1 oz (30 gms) butter
1 oz (30 gms) sugar
3 ¹/₂ oz (100 gms) lemon juice
3 oz (80 gms) apricot jelly

Roll out the pastry dough to a thickness of about 1 ¹/₁₀-in. (3mm) and shape it to line a pie dish. Precook the pastry for 10 minutes in a hot oven (390°F).

In the meantime, prepare the lemon custard. Beat together the eggs, sugar, butter, and lemon juice in a saucepan and boil for 2-3 minutes.

Pour this filling into the tart and cook for 15 minutes in a very hot (430°F) oven.

Allow to cool, then nap with melted apricot jelly.

TARTE TATIN

5 oz (125 gms) butter
9 oz (250 gms) flour
1 egg yolk
¼ cup (5 cl) water
1 oz (30 gms) sugar
½ tsp salt
1 ¾ lbs (750 gms) apples
5 oz (120 gms) sugar
3 oz (80 gms) butter

Mix together butter, flour, egg yolk, water, sugar, and salt in a bowl until they form a soft pastry. Leave for one hour in the refrigerator.

Caramelize the sugar and butter in a pan with a metal handle that can fit in the oven.

Peel, seed, and quarter the apples. Roll out the pastry to a thickness of ¹/₁₀-in. (3 mm). When the caramel is made, lay the pieces of apple in a fan-shape, then lay the pastry on top of them, pinching the edges around the rim of the pan to hold the apples in.

Cook in a very hot oven (430°F) for 40-45 minutes. To remove from the pan, move to a strong heat to melt the caramel, shaking the pan with a gentle circular motion to detach the tart from the pan bottom. Serve warm.

TARTE AUX PRUNES
(Plum Tart)

¾ lb (350 gms) sweet shortcrust pastry
2 ½ oz (70 gms) ground almonds
2 ½ oz (70 gms) sugar
⅝ cup cream
2 eggs
Vanilla
1 lb 2 oz (500 gms) plums
Confectioners sugar

Roll out the dough into a circle ¹/₁₀-in. (3 mm) thick, place it in pie dish, and precook for 10 minutes in a hot oven (390°F).

Prepare the cream filling by mixing the eggs, sugar, cream, milk, vanilla, and ground almonds.

Place the plums in the tart and pour over them half of the above mixture. Cook for 5 minutes and then pour over the other half. Cook for 15-20 minutes.

Leave to cool. Sprinkle with confectioners sugar before serving.

SABAYON

6 eggs
9 oz (250 gms) sugar
1 cup (20 cl) of Sauternes

Whip the six egg yolks with sugar in a bain-marie until stiff. Add Sauternes and continue to whip vigorously over a very low heat until the mixture is frothy and smooth. Serve in a chilled glass or goblet. This is just as good with gin or whisky.

SOUFFLÉ À LA VANILLE
(Vanilla Soufflé)

½ cup (10 cl) milk
1 ½ oz (35 gms) sugar
½ oz (15 gms) flour
1 knob of butter
4 eggs
1 vanilla pod

Boil the milk with the split vanilla pod. Allow to steep for a few minutes, then remove the vanilla. Blend the sugar, flour, and three egg yolks, and mix in the milk; then heat, stirring well, for about two minutes. Remove from the heat and stir in butter.

Whip the four egg whites until stiff and blend them gently into the mixture. Butter the inside of a soufflé dish and sprinkle with sugar; gently add the mixture. Cook for 20 minutes in an oven pre-heated to 350°F; serve piping hot, with a sprinkling of confectioners sugar.

remaining pear juice. Incorporate the cooked sugar, cook all together to 180°F on the refractometer.

When cooked, pour out on a marble slab, in bands between two wooden rulers. Allow to cool, then cut in pieces and roll in the remaining caster sugar.

PÂTE DE COINGS
(Quince Paste Jellies)

3 lbs (1.3 kg) quince
5 oz (125 gms) caster sugar
2 tbsps (25 gms) pectin
3 lbs (1.3 kg) granulated sugar
10 oz (300 gms) glucose
Juice of 1 lemon

In a large saucepan, bring to the boil 3 ½ oz (80 gms) caster sugar, all the granulated sugar, and the lemon juice. When boiling, add the glucose.

Mix the pectin and the quince flesh, and incorporate the sugar; check regularly, stirring with a spatula, and cook to 170°F on the refractometer.

When cooked, pour out on a marble slab in bands between two wooden rulers; allow to cool, then cut in pieces and roll in the remaining caster sugar.

PÂTE DE POMMES VERTES
(Green Apple Paste Jellies)

9 oz (250 gms) caster sugar
3 ¼ lbs (1.5 kg) granulated sugar
7 oz (200 gms) glucose
1 ½ oz (40 gms) pectin
3 ¼ lbs 6 oz (1.5 kg) flesh of green apples
Juice of 1 lemon

In a large saucepan, bring to the boil 5 oz (120 gms) caster sugar and the granulated sugar. When boiling, add the glucose. Mix the pectin and the apples, incorporate this into the sugar; check regularly, stirring with a spatula, and cook to 170°F on the refractometer.

When cooked, pour into a marble slab in bands bewteen two rulers. Allow to cool, then cut in pieces and roll in the remaining caster sugar.

AMBIGU SUCRÉ-SALÉ
(Cold Savories)

The French term *ambigu* means (among other things) an assortment of cold food served as a buffet at a late hour, or otherwise improvised. It can include salty canapés or brochettes made with fruit and other sweet ingredients.

For example, a typical *ambigu* might be composed of a plate of canapés, along with pork rillettes, young asparagus, smoked salmon, hard-boiled eggs, foie gras, roquefort cheese and buttered bread, brochettes of grapefruit and prawns, oranges and gruyère, bacon and prunes.

This is only one assortment among many possibilities; all are delightful both to the palate and to the eye.

AIGUILLONS À BOIRE
(Grilled Sardine Appetizers)

16 small fresh sardines
1 ½ oz (40 gms) mustard
Cayenne pepper
¼ cup (10 cl) eau-de-vie

Grill the sardines, and fillet them. Spread with mustard and powder with cayenne pepper. Place the fillets on a baking dish and put them in a very hot oven for a few minutes; then flambé them in eau-de-vie. Immediately lay them on pieces of toast and serve.

Cold savories.

PORTO À L'AIL
(Port with Garlic)

1 lb garlic
1 bottle vintage port

The medicinal properties of garlic were widely accepted in the Pays d'Oc, but as a rule, oil was used with it instead of port.

Chop the pound of garlic and put in a bottle with vintage port — you will need to drink two glasses of the wine first, to make room for it. Leave to macerate for 20 days.

Start with an evening dose of half a liqueur glass before your soup, then gradually increase to one or two liqueur glasses.

This brew is a sovereign remedy for chronic bron- chitis. Garlic in oil is also an excellent worming dose for children, and in all probability is mortally dangerous to flies.

SARATOGA COCKTAIL

6 drops Angostura bitters
1 liqueur glass Cognac
1 liqueur glass whisky
2 liqueur glasses vermouth (Noilly Prat)

Half fill a cocktail shaker with crushed ice. Add the above ingredients. Mix well and pour into a small wine glass. Serve with a slice of lemon.

CAROLINA SPECIAL COCKTAIL

1 liqueur glass kirsch
1 liqueur glass Gordon's gin
1 liqueur glass Guignolet (cherry liqueur)

Half fill a cocktail shaker with crushed ice. Mix the ingredients together and pour into a cocktail glass with a cherry preserved in eau-de-vie. Serve with short straws.

PORT WINE COBBLER

½ tbsp sugar
1 liqueur glass redcurrant syrup
2 sherry glasses red port

Tip half a tablespoonful of sugar into a shaker. Add the syrup and red port. Fill the shaker with ice; close and shake hard. Pour into glasses and serve with long straws and fresh fruit (cherries, etc).

CLARET COBBLER

In a large glass mix together a teaspoonful of sugar and a sherry glass of water. Add two glasses of red Bordeaux and top up with crushed ice. Stir well with a soda spoon and serve with fresh fruit and long straws.

CHAMPAGNE COBBLER

In a tall glass mix three-quarters of a tablespoon of sugar with a slice of orange and a twist of lemon. Fill the glass three-quarters full with champagne and crushed ice. Stir with a soda spoon and serve with fresh fruit.

LOU PERDIGAT

2 parts Armagnac
2 parts Cointreau
2 parts crème de mûres (blackberry cordial)
4 parts plum juice flavored with coriander

Pour the above ingredients into a glass jug filled with crushed ice. Mix and serve in cocktail glasses. Decorate with fresh coriander, blackberries, or plums.

Recipe by Georges Lestage

ROSALY

3 parts eau-de-vie de framboise (raspberry)
3 parts Cointreau
3 parts crème de banane (banana cordial)
1 part fresh lime juice

Pour the ingredients into a cocktail shaker filled with ice. Shake well and pour into champagne glasses, topping up with very cold champagne. Decorate with a twist of lime and a cherry preserved in eau-de-vie.

Recipe by Georges Lestage

SYLVIA

4 parts pêcher mignon
2 parts vodka
3 parts fresh pineapple juice
1 part wild strawberry liqueur

Add the ingredients to a few ice cubes in a shaker. Close the shaker and shake vigorously, then pour into a tumbler with three ice cubes. Decorate with a strawberry, a slice of fresh pineapple, and fresh mint.

Recipe by Georges Lestage

SAUTERNES COBBLER

In a shaker, pour one teaspoonful of caster sugar, half a sherry glass of grenadine, and two claret glasses of Sauternes. Top up the shaker with crushed ice, close it, and shake well. Serve topped with fresh fruit (e.g. red and white grapes).

WHISKY COBBLER

In a shaker, put one tablespoonful of caster sugar. Add two sherry glasses of Scotch whisky (or bourbon) and one tablespoonful of fresh pineapple juice. Top up the shaker with ice, close, shake well, and serve decorated with fruit (pineapple, or cherries preserved in eau-de-vie).

BRUNSWICK COOLER

This drink should be prepared directly in a tall glass filled with crushed ice. To the juice of half a lemon, add half a glass of caster sugar, and one bottle of ginger ale. Stir well with a spoon and serve.

ROSE COCKTAIL

²/₃ sherry glass gin
¹/₆ sherry glass lemon juice
¹/₃ sherry glass cherry brandy

Fill a mixing glass a quarter full with crushed ice. Mix the above ingredients, strain, and serve immediately in chilled cocktail glasses topped with a cherry preserved in eau-de-vie.

EAST INDIA COCKTAIL

1 teaspoon raspberry syrup
1 teaspoon Curaçao
6 drops Maraschino
1 sherry glass Cognac

Half-fill a mixing glass with crushed ice. Mix the ingredients and pour into a cocktail glass, filling three-quarters full. Top up with champagne and decorate with a twist of lemon.

FANCY BRANDY COCKTAIL

1-3 teaspoons of sugarcane syrup
(according to taste)
2 teaspoons Maraschino
6 drops Angostura bitters
1 sherry glass of Fine Champagne Cognac

Half-fill a mixing glass with crushed ice. Mix the ingredients well and serve in a cocktail glass with a twist of lemon.

OLD TOM COCKTAIL

2 tbsps sugarcane syrup
1 teaspoon Curaçao
6 drops Angostura bitters
1 sherry glass Gordon's gin

Fill a mixing glass three-quarters full with crushed ice. Mix the ingredients well and pour into a cocktail glass; serve with a twist of lemon.

CHAMPAGNE COCKTAIL

1 teaspoon cane syrup
2 teaspoons red Curaçao
6 drops Angostura bitters

Fill a mixing glass one-third full with crushed ice. Add the ingredients, then fill the mixing glass to the top with champagne and stir well. Add half a slice of lemon and half a slice of orange. Pour into a brandy glass, filling three-quarters full.

The original champagne cocktail :
Place in a champagne glass a quarter of a sugar cube soaked in Angostura bitters and a dash of Cognac. Top up with champagne and a twist of lemon.

MACDONALD COCKTAIL

1 teaspoon Curaçao
4 drops Angostura bitters
½ sherry glass Scotch whisky
½ sherry glass Italian vermouth

Fill a mixing glass half full with crushed ice. Mix the ingredients and serve in a cocktail glass.

JULEPS

All juleps are made with crushed fresh mint leaves, to accompany Scotch whisky, bourbon, rye, brandy, rum, etc.
Example : Mint Julep
Crush four or five mint leaves, and mix with a teaspoon of sugar dissolved in a little water in a tumbler and a dash of Angostura bitters.
Fill the tumbler with crushed ice and measures of bourbon whisky, swirling gently until frost forms on the outside of the glass.
Top with a few leaves of mint, half a slice of orange, half a slice of lemon, and a candied cherry.

VERMOUTH CUP

In a large jug, dissolve 4 oz sugar in a little soda water. Add half a cup of Cointreau, half a cup of Grand Marnier, one cup of Armagnac, fruits in season sliced thin, and a bottle of vermouth.
Stir and allow to stand for 20 minutes in the refrigerator before serving in large wine glasses. Take care not to damage the fruit.

DRY MARTINI

In a mixing glass, combine ice, two parts dry vermouth, and eight parts gin. Stir and pour into a chilled cocktail glass, with a twist of lemon or an olive. Vodka may be substituted for the gin.

A.M.B.A.

4 parts Scotch whisky
3 parts navy rum
3 parts red vermouth
1 part Cointreau

Mix in a glass with ice and decorate with a slice of lemon and a Maraschino cherry.

MANHATTAN

In a mixing glass add to ice a few drops of Angostura bitters, three parts Italian vermouth, and seven parts rye whiskey.
Stir and pour into a chilled cocktail glass, decorating with a cherry preserved in eau-de-vie.

GIBSON

In a mixing glass, combine ice, two parts dry vermouth, and eight parts gin. Stir and serve in a chilled cocktail glass with a couple of white pickled onions.

NEGRONI

In an ice-filled tumbler, combine equal quantities of Italian vermouth, Campari, and gin, with half a slice of lemon. Decorate with a twist of lemon and half a slice of orange.

MARGARITA

In a shaker, combine the juice of a lime, one part Cointreau, and two parts tequila. Add crushed ice, shake hard, and serve in a cocktail glass with the rim frosted with salt.

BULLSHOT

In a tumbler, mix ice cubes, a dash of lemon juice, twice as much Worcester sauce, salt, pepper, Tabasco, and a measure of vodka. Top up with cold beef consommé and serve.

MARTINI COCKTAIL

Fill a mixing glass half full with crushed ice. Add a teaspoon sugarcane syrup, six drops of Angostura bitters, a third of a sherry glass of gin, and half a sherry glass of Noilly Prat. Mix the ingredients thoroughly and serve in a cocktail glass. You can obviously alter the proportions to make a dryer martini, eliminating the cane syrup and augmenting the dose of gin.

BRANDY PUNCH

¹/₂ sherry glass lemon juice
¹/₄ sherry glass rum
1 ¹/₂ sherry glasses Cognac
1 piece fresh pineapple
2 slices orange

Put a tablespoon of sugar in a large glass. Add the ingredients, then top up the glass with crushed ice and stir well with a spoon.

RUSSIAN CUP

For twenty-five people :
3 bottles red claret (or Malromé, even better)
2 cups Curaçao
2 ¹/₂ cups sherry
2 ¹/₂ cups brandy
2 wine glasses raspberry syrup
3 sliced oranges with the pips removed
1 sliced lemon with the pips removed
4 sprigs fresh green mint
2 siphons soda water
3 bottles soda

Mix together in a large bowl with a ladle, sweeten to taste, and leave to stand for an hour. Then pour into another bowl filled with crushed ice and serve in small wine glasses.

CHAMPAGNE PUNCH

1 liqueur glass lemon juice
1 liqueur glass strawberry syrup
1 slice orange
¹/₂ slice pineapple
Champagne

Put half a tablespoon of sugar in a large glass. Add the ingredients. Half-fill a large glass with crushed ice and top up with champagne. Mix gently, so the champagne does not lose its fizz.
Extra fruit can be added according to taste.

CRIMEAN CUP

For eight people :
2 ¹/₂ cups orgeat syrup
³/₄ cup brandy

¹/₂ cup white rum
1 bottle champagne
1 bottle soda
4 oz sugar
2 sliced lemons with pips removed
2 sliced oranges with pips removed
6 slices fresh pineapple

Mix the ingredients with a ladle in a large jug and transfer to another jar half full of crushed ice. Serve in small wine glasses.

CHAMPAGNE CUP

For twenty people :
2 ¹/₂ cups brandy
2 ¹/₂ cups Curaçao
2 ¹/₂ cups Tokay wine
1 ¹/₄ cups green Chartreuse
1 wine glass pineapple syrup
3 sprigs fresh lemon balm
3 sliced oranges, with pips removed
1 sliced lemon, with pips removed
2 bottles sparkling water

Mix well in a large bowl with a ladle. Cover the bowl with a cloth and allow to stand for at least 2 hours. Then pour into a salad bowl or silver punch-bowl and add half a fresh pineapple cut in slices and three bottles of ice-cold champagne.

Place your bowl in an ice bucket, bedding it in crushed ice, and serve as cold as possible in wine glasses.

PORT FLIP

Into a shaker three-quarters filled with crushed ice, pour a whole beaten egg, a tablespoon of sugar, and a sherry glass of red port. Close the shaker, shake well, pour into a brandy glass. Sprinkle with a little ground nutmeg and serve.

ROCKY COOLER

Into a large glass, pour an egg, half a tablespoon of sugar, and the juice of a lemon. Beat until the mixture is nearly white, then add five or six ice cubes. Top up with cider, shake, sprinkle with nutmeg, and serve.

EGGNOG

Fill a shaker one-third full with crushed ice. Add a whole egg, a tablespoon of sugar, and a wine glass of whisky. Top up with unpasteurized milk. Close the shaker, shake well, pour the mixture into a wine glass, and sprinkle with ground nutmeg.

IMPERIAL EGG NOG

1 tbsp sugar
1 egg
1 sherry glass brandy
1 sherry glass rum

In a shaker one-third full of crushed ice, mix the ingredients. Top up with unpasteurized milk, shake well, pour into a tall glass, sprinkle with nutmeg, and serve.

GLORY FIZZ

In a shaker, dissolve a tablespoon of sugar in the juice of half a lemon. Add one egg white, two teaspoons of Pernod, and a small wine glass of Scotch whisky. Add crushed ice and top up with soda. Close the shaker, shake well, serve and drink immediately.

SILVER FIZZ

Pour half a tablespoon of sugar and two teaspoons of lemon juice into a shaker. Stir with a spoon until the sugar dissolves, then add one egg white and a wine glass of gin. Top up with crushed ice, close the shaker, shake well, and pour into a tall glass, with a dash of seltzer water to complete.

DERBY COCKTAIL

Fill a shaker two-thirds full with ice. Add half a tablespoon of sugar, two sherry glasses of Amontillado sherry, and a liqueur glass of pineapple syrup. Close the shaker, shake hard, and pour into a tall glass. Decorate with two slices of fresh pineapple and four strawberries, over which you should pour (*without mixing*) a liqueur glass of red port.

FRUIT COCKTAIL

6 drops Angostura bitters
1 sherry glass orange juice
1 sherry glass lemon juice
1 sherry glass grapefruit juice
1 or 2 teaspoons sugarcane syrup (to taste)

Half-fill a mixing glass with crushed ice. Add the ingredients, mix well and serve in a wine glass.

JERSEY COCKTAIL

½ tbsp sugar
6 drops Angostura bitters
1 sherry glass cider

In a mixing glass, place four or five ice cubes. Add the ingredients, mix well, and pour into a chilled cocktail glass. Add a twist of lemon and serve with small straws.

OMNIUM COCKTAIL

2 teaspoons sugarcane syrup
4 drops Angostura bitters
6 drops Maraschino
1 sherry glass vermouth

Half-fill a mixing glass with crushed ice. Add the ingredients, mix well, and pour into a chilled cocktail glass, add a twist of lemon, and serve.

SHERRY COBBLER

1 tbsp sugar
1 liqueur glass brandy
1 liqueur glass Curaçao
2 sherry glasses dry sherry

Fill the shaker two-thirds full of crushed ice. Add the ingredients, close the shaker, and shake well, then pour into a tall glass. Decorate the cobbler with two slices of orange, and over these pour, *without mixing*, a liqueur glass of red port.

HOLY WATER

Boil together half a glass of rosewater, half a glass of sour wine (verjuice), a little fresh ginger, and a little fresh marjoram. Strain and drink.

GLOSSARY

bain-marie : a vessel usually half-filled with near-boiling hot water in which sauces and dishes can be cooked slowly or kept warm; in the U.S., a double boiler.

blanch : to dip in boiling water for a few minutes, thereby tenderizing meat and removing bitter flavors from vegetables.

bouquet garni : aromatic herbs or plants (usually parsley, thyme, and bay leaf) tied together in a small bunch, cooked with stews and sauces. Discard before serving.

braise : to cook in an airtight pan over a low heat, adding very little water.

brunoise : vegetables diced and cooked in the same way as a mirepoix, but using butter instead of pork fat. Used for flavoring shellfish dishes.

chinois : a conical utensil for filtering sauces.

court-bouillon : an aromatic liquor of water boiled with carrots, onions, bouquet garni, and white wine, which is used to cook meat, fish, or vegetables.

crème fraîche : matured cream in which lactic acids and the natural process of fermentation have caused the cream to thicken and take on a nutty flavor. *Not sour cream;* sour cream with 18 to 20 percent butterfat content is no substitute, since it cannot be boiled without curdling. Use double cream with a butterfat content of at least 30 per cent.

deglaze : to liquefy the caramelized juices remaining on the bottom of a saucepan or other cooking pan by adding a liquid (such as wine, stock, or water).

degrease : to skim off the grease from the top of a cooked preparation with a ladle.

demi-glace : strictly speaking, a brown sauce made by boiling and skimming an espagnole sauce base and mixing in white sauce, estouffade, or clear soup.

eau-de-vie : an alcoholic liquid with an alcohol content of 16° to 17° proof. The term covers distilled wine (brandy), and spirits distilled from fruit and cereals.

étamine : like a chinois, but with a much finer straining effect.

foie gras frais : the fresh uncooked liver of a force-fed duck or goose.

foie gras demi-cuit : fresh force-fed duck or goose liver cooked in a bain-marie until pink.

julienne : a clear vegetable soup made from consommé, to which are added finely shredded vegetables cooked very slowly in butter until tender. A julienne can also mean any finely shredded foodstuff.

mirepoix : a mixture of diced carrots, onions, celery, and a little thyme and bay leaf, cooked slowly with raw ham, pork fat, or butter, and used as a flavor-enhancer for meat, fish, and shellfish dishes.

quatre épices : a mixture of white pepper, powdered cloves, ginger, and nutmeg.

reduce : to concentrate a liquid by boiling away part of it.

roux : the thickening element in sauces, a mixture of butter or other fatty substances and flour, cooked together for varying lengths of time depending on the use to be made of it.

salamandre : a gas-heated oven, into which dishes are put to brown or glaze very quickly.

Index of the recipes

Index

INDEX OF PLACES

Dwellings

Place names

Galleries and dealers

Cafés, restaurants, and places of entertainment

Select bibliography

ADLER, Laure, *La Vie quotidienne dans les maisons closes, 1830-1930*. Paris, 1991.

ATTEMS, comtesse, *Notre oncle Lautrec*. 1990.

BEAUTÉ, Georges, *Toulouse-Lautrec vu par les photographes*. Lausanne, 1988.

BERNIER, Georges, *La Revue blanche*. Paris, 1991.

COOPER, Douglas, *Henri de Toulouse-Lautrec*. Paris, 1963.

DEVOISINS, Jean, *L'Univers de Toulouse-Lautrec*. Paris, 1980.

DEVYNCK, Danièle, *Toulouse-Lautrec*. Paris, 1992.

DORTU, M.-G., *La Cuisine de Toulouse-Lautrec et de Maurice Joyant*. Lausanne, 1964.

DUROZOI, Gérard, *Toulouse-Lautrec*. Paris, 1992.

FERMIGIER, André, *Toulouse-Lautrec*. Paris, 1991.

GAUZI, François, *Lautrec, mon ami*. Paris, 1992.

HUISMAN, P. and M.G. DORTU, *Lautrec by Lautrec*. Edited by Corinne Bellow. Newbury Books.

JOYANT, Maurice, *La Cuisine de Monsieur Momo, célibataire*. Paris, 1930.

JOYANT, Maurice, *Henri de Toulouse-Lautrec, 1864-1901*. 2 vols. Ayer Company Publishers, Inc., 1968 (reprint of 1927 edition).

LASSAIGNE, Jacques, *Lautrec*. Lausanne, 1953.

LECLERCQ, Paul, *Autour de Toulouse-Lautrec*. Genève, 1954.

NATANSON, Thadée, *Un Henri de Toulouse-Lautrec*. Genève, 1951.

PERRUCHOT, Henri, *La Vie de Toulouse-Lautrec*. Paris, 1958.

RODAT, Charles de, *Toulouse-Lautrec, Album de famille*. Paris, 1985.

SIMON, Alfred, *Toulouse-Lautrec*. Paris, 1990.

TOULOUSE-LAUTREC, Henri de, *The Letters of Henri de Toulouse-Lautrec*. Edited by Herbert D. Schimmel. Oxford University Press, Inc., 1991.

TOULOUSE-LAUTREC, comte de, *Le Peintre Henri de Toulouse-Lautrec et son entourage familial*. Text of the speech given to the Académie des Jeux floraux in Toulouse, March 20, 1990.

Catalogs and collective works

Toulouse-Lautrec, catalog of the exhibition at Grand Palais, Paris, Feb. 18-June 1, 1992.

Toulouse-Lautrec, collection *Le Temps*, Paris, 1991.

Toulouse-Lautrec, prince de la nuit, catalog Muséart, Paris, 1992.

Toulouse-Lautrec et ses amis, catalog of the exhibition at Musée Toulouse-Lautrec, Albi, March 21-May 31, 1992.

Toulouse-Lautrec et le Japonisme, catalog of the exhibition at Musée Toulouse-Lautrec, Albi, June 29-September 1, 1991.

Enfance de Toulouse-Lautrec, 1864-1882. Excerpted from *La Revue du Tarn*, n° 145. Albi, spring 1992. Exhibition organised by the Association pour la sauvegarde du Vieil Alby.

List of paintings, drawings and lithographs

PRINCETEAU, René

15   Henri de Toulouse-Lautrec, his father and Princeteau, drawing. Musée Toulouse-Lautrec, Albi.

TOULOUSE-LAUTREC, Henri de

8   *Au Bar*, 1887, oil on canvas, 55,2 × 41,9 cm. The Virginia Museum of Fine arts, Paul Mellon collection.

12   *Comtesse Alphonse de Toulouse-Lautrec*, 1882, oil on canvas, 41 × 32 cm. Musée Toulouse-Lautrec, Albi.

44   *Submersion*, 1881, pen and ink, 18 × 23 cm. House where Toulouse-Lautrec was born, Albi.

56   *Étude de nu*, 1883, oil on canvas, 55 × 46 cm. Musée Toulouse-Lautrec, Albi.

62   *Le Repos du modèle*, 1889, oil on cardboard. J. Paul Getty Museum, Malibu.

71   *Invitation à une tasse de lait*, 1897, lithograph with pencil, 38 × 25 cm. Bibliothèque nationale, Paris.

75   *Autoportrait*, 1882-1883, oil on wood, 40,5 × 32,5 cm. Musée Toulouse-Lautrec, Albi.

78   *Tapir le scélérat*, drawing. Private collection.
       Un interne : monsieur Gabriel Tapié de Céleyran, 1894, pen and ink on tinted paper, 33 × 22 cm. Musée Toulouse-Lautrec, Albi.

84   *La Passagère du 54*, 1896, lithograph with brush, spit and pencil, 60 × 40 cm. Musée de la Publicité, Paris.

86   *Le Crocodile*, 1896, lithograph with brush. Private collection.

87   Invitation to a party given by Alexandre Natanson at 60, avenue du Bois, 1895, lithograph with brush and pencil, with words added by a different hand, 25,6 × 15,5 cm. Musée Toulouse-Lautrec, Albi.

90   *À table chez M. et Mme Thadée Natanson*, 1895, oil, gouache and pastel on cardboard, 57,2 × 78,1 cm. The Museum of Fine Arts, Houston.

96   *La Revue blanche*, 1895, lithograph with brush, spit and pencil, 125,5 × 91,2 cm. Private collection.

98   *Suzanne Valadon*, 1886-1887, oil on canvas, 54,4 × 45 cm, Ny Carlsberg Glyptotek, Copenhague.

107   Study for *Femme tirant son bas*, circa 1894, oil on canvas, 61,5 × 44,5 cm. Musée Toulouse-Lautrec, Albi.

111   *Les Deux amies*, 1895, oil on cardboard, 45,5 × 67,5 cm. Private collection.

113   *Débauche*, 1896, lithograph with brush, spit and pencil, 24,4 x 32,3 cm. Private collection.

117   *Ces Dames au réfectoire*, 1893-1894, oil on cardboard. Svépmüveszeti Museum, Budapest.

122   *L'Anglais au Moulin-Rouge*, 1892, lithograph with brush and spit, 63 × 49 cm. Musée Toulouse-Lautrec, Albi.

123   Yvette Guilbert between Oscard Wilde and Toulouse-Lautrec, 1895, drawing. Musée de Pontoise.

124   Study for *Moulin Rouge - La Goulue*, 1891, charcoal, stump, pastel, wash and oil on tinted paper, remounted on canvas, 154 × 118 cm. Musée Toulouse-Lautrec, Albi.

125   *Gin cocktail*, 1886. Collection Georges Beaute.

128   *La Clownesse assise* (Cha-U-Kao), 1896, lithograph with brush, spit and pencil. Private collection.

List of photographs

Acknowledgments

I extend my heartfelt thanks to Anne Roquebert, keeper at the Musée d'Orsay, whom I met at a lunch arranged by Marie Déqué. Her fascinating account of Toulouse-Lautrec's way of life gave me the idea for a book based on his relish of good food. I am also indebted to Daphné de Saint-Sauveur for her support and Anne Robin for her invaluable advice. Among those who helped me put together this book, I owe special thanks to Jim Palette, a remarkable « coach » ; to Jean-Pierre de Guibert and Paul Dumas-Ricord, who opened their library to me ; to Christine Barbaste, who helped my bibliographical researches ; and Franck Bayard, whose practical assistance was enormous.

My thanks to André Daguin, whose culinary choices and advice could not have failed to enthuse Lautrec.

My deep gratitude to Mademoiselle Nicole Tapié de Céleyran, who welcomed me at the Château du Bosc and, unsparing with her time and her enthusiasm, exquisitely recreated the world of the painter's family.

My greatest thanks go to the Comte de Toulouse-Lautrec, an unrivaled source of information on his family ; to Danièle Devynck, keeper at the Toulouse-Lautrec Museum at Albi, for the interest she took in this book ; to Bérangère Desplas, in charge of the museum's information office.
I want also to thank Madame Dominique de Rostolan and Messieurs Georges Beaute, Paul Nollevalle, Charles de Rodat, and the Ombres Blanches bookshop at Toulouse.

Geneviève Diego-Dortignac

The realization of a book like this is long and complicated ; it requires the help of many hands.
My thanks go to all the team of Editions Scala and to David Campbell who has, for many years, placed his trust in me.
And to three women in particular :
Mademoiselle Nicole Tapié de Céleyran, whose enthusiasm and kindness made our visits to the Château du Bosc such happy occasions.
Lydia Fasoli, who gave me untiring support throughout the project.
Lastly, to Sylvie Raulet who kept alive, in all of us, over the months, the originality and exoticism of the character we were seeking to present.

Jean-Bernard Naudin

Acknowledgments

My warmest thanks go to Jean-Bernard Naudin for his faith in the project and his suggestions, which benefited the entire team.

My gratitude is due also to Sylvie Raulet and Jean-Pascal Billaud.

And to Véronique Ardant, Lavinia Salmon, Thomas Huyghues Despointes, Bruno and Mustapha, whose good temper and efficiency were of great help.

My thanks to all those who received us, Nicole Tapié de Céleyran, Céline Armagnac, Frédérique Mistral, Françoise Monnier, Yolande Tapié de Céleyran, Galiane et Louis de Saint Palais. The management of the Opéra Comique, Salle Favart. Yves Tranier, keeper at the Musée d'histoire naturelle, Jardin des Plantes. The advice of Jean-Louis Riccardi and Pierre Breton des Loÿs was invaluable.

My utmost thanks to the following galleries and antique dealers : Anne Vincent ; Catherine Arigoni ; Art domestique ancien ; Art d'autrefois ; Association nationale des fauconniers ; Au Bain Marie ; Aux fils du Temps ; Michèle Baconnier ; Fréha, Christian Benais ; Alexandre Biaggi ; les Bijoux, Louvre des Antiquaires ; Marie-Pierre Boitard ; Bernard Captier ; Cazal, Puces Marché Serpette ; Annick Clavier ; Chotard ; Cochelin, Louvre des Antiquaires ; Daulliac ; Marie-Claude Delahaye ; les Deux Orphelines ; Valérie, Patrick Divers ; Éric Dubois ; Duprey, Dîner en Ville ; Fanette ; la Faucille d'or, Carré d'or ; le Faucon ; Fréha ; Fuchsia ; Jeanne Gambert de Loche ; Muriel Grateau ; Garance ; Galerie Elstir ; Galerie J. Coti ; Galerie Dominique Paramythiotis ; les Indiennes, tissus anciens ; Jardin Imaginaire ; Kimonoya ; Laure Lombardini ; l'Or du Temps ; Dorothée d'Orgeval ; Point à la ligne ; Portobello ; Christian Sapet, Puces marché Serpette ; Siècle ; Suissa, Carré d'Or ; Summum ; Surger, Louvre des Antiquaires ; la Vie de Château ; Vivement Jeudi ; Laure Welfling.

Lydia Fasoli

Editions Scala thanks the Gorne laboratory for the development of the photographs and Jacques Renault Dunbar for the pastiches of works reproduced in this book.

Photographic credits

Georges Beaute : 14, 48, 69, 70, 85, 125. Bibliothèque nationale, Paris : 54, 71. Giraudon : 123. J. Paul Getty Museum, Malibu : 62. Josefowitz Collection : 134. Toulouse-Lautrec's house : 44. Ny Carlsberg Glyptotek, Copenhagen : 98. Musée de la Publicité : 84, 138. Charles de Rodat : 32. Roger-Viollet : 45, 47, 120, 122. Svépmuveszeti Museum, Budapest : 117. The Museum of The Fine Arts, Houston : 90. Toulouse-Lautrec's Museum, Albi : 11, 12, 15, 56, 74, 75, 77, 78, 87, 107, 122, 124, 133. Rights reserved for all other documents.

Typeset by Charente Photogravure
Colour origination by Daïchi Process & Jovis - Paris
Printed by Mohndruck - Germany